How to Self-Publish on a Budget

*Everything You Need to Write, Edit,
And Launch Your Book for
Little or No Cost*

Fee O'Shea

Published by: White Rockit Books
© 2025 by Fee O'Shea

All Rights Reserved.
No part of this publication may be reproduced in any form or by any means, including printing, scanning, photocopying, or otherwise, without prior written permission of the copyright holder.
Terms of Use
You are given a non-transferable, "personal use" license to this product. You cannot distribute it or share it with other individuals.

Additionally, no resale rights or private label rights are granted when purchasing this document. In other words, it's for your own personal use only.

First published: 2025
ISBN 978-0-473-76528-6

Acknowledge:
I want to acknowledge the assistance of ChatGPT, whose research support and editorial insights significantly contributed to the clarity and accessibility of this book.

How to Self-Publish on a Budget

Table of Contents

Introduction – Yes, You Can Self-Publish

Chapter 1 – Getting Started

- Why Write a Book? Clarifying Your Purpose
- Choosing Your Genre
- Who Is Your Reader?
- Outlining Your Book (Fiction and Nonfiction)

Chapter 2 – The Writing Process

- The First Draft Mindset
- Using AI as an Assistant (Not a Replacement)
- Best Practices for Co-Writing with AI
- Overcoming Writer's Block

Chapter 3 – Editing Your Manuscript

- Types of Editing (Developmental, Line, Copy, Proof)
- DIY Editing Tools and Techniques
- When to Read Out Loud
- Knowing When to Hire an Editor (and Budget Options)

Chapter 4 – Formatting and Layout

- DIY Benefits of Formatting
- Formatting for eBooks
- Formatting for Print (Trim Sizes, Templates, Margins)
- Common Formatting Mistakes to Avoid

Chapter 5 – ISBNs and Metadata

- Do You Need an ISBN?
- Free vs Own ISBN: Pros and Cons
- How Metadata Helps Readers Find Your Book
- Step-by-Step: Getting Your ISBN on a Budget

Chapter 6 – Cover Design

- Why Covers Matter
- Tips for Eye-Catching Covers
- Canva, AI, and Templates
- Testing Covers with Your Audience

Chapter 7 – Publishing Platforms

- Amazon KDP: Step by Step
- Other Retailers (Apple, Kobo, B&N, Google Play, IngramSpark)
- Aggregators (Draft2Digital, Smashwords, PublishDrive)
- Exclusivity vs Wide Distribution

Chapter 8 – Pricing and Royalties

- How Royalties Work on Amazon KDP
- Pricing Strategies (Fiction & Nonfiction)
- Promotions and Kindle Unlimited
- Tracking and Adjusting

Chapter 9 – Marketing Your Book

- Building Your Author Brand
- Social Media for Authors
- Free and Low-Cost Marketing Strategies
- Social Media: Free vs Paid Ads
- A Simple Marketing Plan

Chapter 10 – The Long Game: Building a Publishing Career

- Why More Than One Book Matters
- Planning Your Next Project
- Building Sustainable Writing Habits
- Balancing Creativity and Business

Conclusion – Your Words Matter

Proofreading Checklist

About the Author

How to Self-Publish on a Budget

Introduction - Yes, You Can Self-Publish

Have you ever dreamed of seeing your name on the cover of a book? For many aspiring authors, that dream has felt out of reach, locked away behind the gates of traditional publishing houses and lengthy submission processes. The good news is that times have changed. Today, thanks to digital technology and online publishing platforms, you no longer need to wait for a literary agent's approval or a publisher's acceptance letter. You can self-publish your book and share your story with the world—quickly, affordably, and on your own terms.

Self-publishing has opened the door for thousands of writers across the globe. From hobbyists who simply want to leave a legacy for their family, to entrepreneurs using books to build authority, to novelists eager to reach readers directly—it's a world of possibilities. Best of all, you don't need to spend thousands of dollars to make it happen. With the right tools, knowledge, and a little determination, you can publish a professional-quality book for very little cost.

This book is designed for budding authors who want to avoid common pitfalls, cut through the confusion, and learn a straightforward path to self-publishing. We'll explore the entire process step by step:

- **Writing your manuscript** – Whether you're going it alone, using AI tools as your assistant, or even leaning on AI to help generate content, you'll learn the options available and how to make them work for you.
- **Editing** – Discover when and how to self-edit, when it's worth getting professional help, and the difference between types of editing.
- **Formatting and design** – From structuring your eBook for Kindle to preparing a paperback version, we'll look at free and low-cost options.
- **Publishing requirements** – What you need to know about ISBNs, metadata, and distribution formats.

- **Publishing platforms** – We'll explore both retail outlets like Amazon Kindle Direct Publishing and aggregators that can distribute to multiple stores for you.
- **Marketing and beyond** – How to spread the word, build your author brand, and expand into other formats like audiobooks.

Along the way, you'll also learn how to avoid common traps, such as vanity publishers and unnecessary expenses.

By the end of this book, you'll have a clear roadmap from blank page to published work—without wasting time, money, or energy.

So, whether you're writing a memoir, a children's book, a novel, or a practical guide, this is your invitation to step into the exciting world of self-publishing. Your book deserves to be read, and the tools to make it happen are right at your fingertips.

Chapter 1 - Getting Started

Every book begins with an idea. Sometimes it sneaks up on you in the middle of the night, a scene or a character so vivid you have to scribble it down before it vanishes. Other times it's more of a slow simmer, a thought that's been living quietly in the back of your mind for months or even years. Inspiration doesn't really care where you are—you might be washing the dishes, walking on the beach, or standing in line at the supermarket when it taps you on the shoulder and whispers, *"This could be a book."*

Wherever and however your idea arrives, it's precious. This spark is what will carry you through the ups and downs of the writing and publishing journey. There will be days when the words flow and days when you'd rather reorganise the sock drawer than write a single sentence. Coming back to that original spark—the story you wanted to tell, the message you wanted to share—will help you push forward.

But before you leap into typing your first chapter at lightning speed, it's worth pausing to take stock. Think of it as drawing a map before setting off on a road trip. If you know your starting point and your destination, the journey becomes much smoother. Two simple questions will help:

1. **Why am I writing this book?**
   Is it to entertain, to teach, to inspire, or to leave a legacy? Being clear about your "why" will keep you anchored when motivation wobbles.
2. **Who am I writing it for?**
   Picture your ideal reader. What are they interested in? What tone will resonate with them? If you're writing a guide, what problem are you helping them solve? If it's fiction, what kind of adventure or escape are they looking for?

Taking the time to answer these questions at the beginning will save you from headaches later. It will guide your writing style, help you decide on the format, and make your book far easier to market when the time comes. Skipping this step is a bit like setting out on a hike without checking the weather—you might still get there, but you'll be caught off guard along the way.

So, grab a notebook (or open a new document) and jot down a few sentences about your purpose and your reader. This little exercise is the foundation that will support everything else you build.

Why Write a Book? Clarifying Your Purpose

Not all books are written for the same reasons, and that's part of the beauty of self-publishing—*your* reason is valid. Some people dream of becoming the next big name in fiction, while others simply want to put their memories down for their grandchildren to read one day. The key is to know *your* purpose before you begin, because that purpose will guide many of your decisions along the way.

Here are some common reasons people write books:

- **To share personal experiences or family history.**
  Maybe you've lived through an extraordinary event, or you want to preserve family stories before they're lost to time. A memoir or family history doesn't have to be a bestseller to be valuable—it's a gift to the people who matter most.
- **To establish authority in a field.**
  Coaches, consultants, health professionals, business owners—many use books as a way to showcase their expertise. A published book acts like a business card on steroids. It can help attract clients, secure speaking opportunities, and position you as an expert in your niche.
- **To entertain, inspire, or thrill readers.**
  Novelists and storytellers write to bring characters to life, whisk readers away to new worlds, or spark emotions that linger long after the last page. Fiction has its own rewards: connecting with readers through imagination and creativity.
- **To create a legacy.**
  Some people write so that their children, grandchildren, or future generations will know their story. It might never sit on a bookstore shelf, but it will live on as part of the family's history—a treasure far beyond financial value.

Your purpose matters because it shapes everything that follows—your writing style, the length and format of your book, even how you promote it once it's finished. Writing for fun, for example, is very different from writing to build a business or aiming for bestseller status.

There's no "wrong" reason to write a book. But knowing your *why* gives you two big advantages:

1. **Clarity.** You'll make decisions more easily because you'll have a compass pointing you in the right direction.
2. **Motivation.** When writing feels tough (and it will, at times), reminding yourself of your *why* will keep you moving forward.

Here's a quick exercise: grab a piece of paper and finish this sentence—

"I want to write this book because…"

Don't overthink it. Write whatever comes to mind. That single sentence can become your anchor through the writing and publishing process.

Choosing Your Genre and Audience

Once you've clarified *why* you're writing, the next step is to figure out *what* kind of book you're creating and *who* it's for. This might sound obvious ("I'm writing a romance novel" or "I'm writing a guide to gardening"), but getting specific now will make your life much easier later.

Think of genre and audience as two sides of the same coin:

- **Genre** tells you where your book fits on the shelf.
- **Audience** tells you who will be most excited to pick it up.

What Genre Are You Writing In?

Genres are like labels that help readers (and bookshops, and online stores) know what to expect. When someone picks up a romance novel, they expect a love story. If they grab a thriller, they expect suspense, danger, and twists. The same is true for nonfiction—if a reader buys a cookbook, they're looking for recipes, not a memoir about travel.

Here are some examples of popular genres:

- **Fiction:** Romance, thriller, mystery, fantasy, historical fiction, science fiction, literary fiction, children's books.
- **Nonfiction:** Memoir, biography, self-help, health and wellness, business, travel, cookbooks, spirituality, how-to guides.

Your book may cross boundaries (for instance, a historical romance, or a memoir with self-help lessons), but it's still important to know your *primary* genre. Why? Because readers are drawn to clear promises. A thriller reader will be disappointed if your story has no suspense, just as a business reader will be puzzled if your "how-to" book wanders into personal anecdotes without any practical tips.

Think of genre as the "home shelf" for your book—both in a physical bookstore and on Amazon. It's where your ideal reader will go looking. If your book is sitting in the wrong section, it may never find the readers it deserves.

So, ask yourself:

- What is the main experience I'm promising my reader? (Romance? Fear? Adventure? Practical advice?)
- If my book were in a bookstore, what section would I expect to find it in?

Quick Genre Checklist:
To test if you've chosen the right genre, try this:

1. **Find five bestselling books** in the category you think yours belongs to.
2. **Compare their covers and titles**—do they look and sound like the type of book you're writing?
3. **Check the blurbs**—do they highlight the same themes, tone, or promises as your book?
4. **Ask yourself**—if your book sat beside these five, would a reader see it as part of the same family?

If the answer is yes, you've likely chosen the right genre. If not, you may need to rethink where your book belongs.

Who Is Your Ideal Reader?

Once you've settled on your genre, the next question is: *who exactly are you writing for?* Many new authors say, "My book is for everyone!" but in reality, no book appeals to everyone. Trying to please the whole world usually makes your book feel vague and unfocused.

Instead, picture your ideal reader as one specific person. Imagine them walking into a bookstore (or browsing Amazon) and choosing your book over thousands of others. What made them click? What are they hoping to get out of it?

Here are some ways to define your ideal reader:

- **Age group**: Children, teens, young adults, adults, or seniors.
- **Life stage**: Students, new parents, professionals, retirees.
- **Interests**: Romance fans, fantasy lovers, entrepreneurs, health-conscious readers, hobby enthusiasts.
- **Challenges or desires**: Do they want to solve a problem, learn something new, or escape into a story world?

For example:

- A **romance author** might picture a woman in her 30s who reads to relax after work and loves happily-ever-afters.
- A **business coach** might write for solo entrepreneurs who want clear, practical advice without jargon.
- A **memoir writer** might aim for readers who enjoy inspiring, real-life stories with lessons woven in.

When you know your ideal reader, you can tailor your writing style, tone, and even cover design to match what they're looking for. It also helps later with marketing—you'll know which social media platforms to focus on, what kind of keywords to use, and where to find your audience.

Quick Exercise:
Close your eyes and imagine your ideal reader holding your book. Then, answer these questions in a notebook:

1. What age and stage of life are they in?
2. What do they enjoy reading (or what problem are they hoping to solve)?
3. What will they gain, feel, or experience by reading your book?

Try writing a short "reader profile" in two or three sentences. For example:

"My ideal reader is a woman in her 40s who loves cosy mysteries. She wants light, engaging stories that whisk her away after a long day at work, with characters she can cheer for and puzzles that keep her guessing."

Having this picture in mind keeps your writing focused and your book more likely to connect with the right people.

Why This Matters

Being clear about genre and audience will influence:

- The tone and style of your writing.
- The cover design (romance covers look very different from business guides).
- The keywords and categories you choose when publishing.
- How you promote your book later.

When you know who you're writing for, your book will feel more focused—and your readers will feel like you wrote it just for them.

Quick Exercise:
On a fresh page of your notebook, jot down:

1. My book's genre is _____.
2. My ideal reader is _____ (describe them in one or two sentences).
3. My book will give this reader _____ (knowledge, entertainment, hope, escape, etc.).

This little profile becomes your guiding star for everything that follows.

The Myth vs. Reality of Self-Publishing

Self-publishing has exploded in recent years, but with that growth comes a fair bit of misunderstanding. Some people see it as a "shortcut," while others dismiss it as second-best to traditional publishing. The truth sits somewhere in between.

Let's bust a few of the most common myths:

Myth 1: "If I put my book on Amazon, readers will magically find it."

- **Reality:** Amazon is a massive bookstore with millions of titles. Simply uploading your book is like placing one copy on the bottom shelf of a giant library and hoping someone stumbles across it. The good news is that Amazon *does* give indie authors powerful tools—keywords, categories, promotions—but you'll need to use them wisely. Marketing matters just as much as the writing.

Myth 2: "Self-publishing is only for people who couldn't get a 'real' publishing deal."

- **Reality:** That might have been the stigma years ago, but not anymore. Many successful authors *choose* self-publishing because it gives them freedom, speed, and control. Big-name writers like Hugh Howey (*Wool*) and Colleen Hoover (*Slammed*) started out self-publishing before landing major deals. Others stay independent because the royalties are higher and they keep the rights to their work.

Myth 3: "It costs a fortune to self-publish."

- **Reality:** It *can* cost a lot if you outsource everything—editing, design, marketing—but it doesn't have to. With free tools, clever DIY, and even some help from AI, you can produce a professional-quality book on a shoestring budget. The biggest investment is your time and effort.

Myth 4: "Self-published books don't make money."

- **Reality:** While it's true that not every book becomes a bestseller (the same is true in traditional publishing!), plenty of indie authors earn a steady income. Some treat it as a side hustle, others as a full-time career. Success depends on writing consistently, understanding your audience, and learning a little about marketing.

So What's the Reality?

Self-publishing is both empowering and demanding. You get to call the shots—when to publish, what your cover looks like, how to price your book—but you also take on responsibilities that a traditional publisher would normally handle, like editing, formatting, and promotion.

The payoff? You're in control. You can move quickly, experiment, learn from mistakes, and hold your published book in your hands without waiting months (or years) for approval from a publisher.

Quick Reflection:
Ask yourself: *"Am I ready to treat this like a learning process, not just a one-time upload?"*
If you can approach self-publishing with curiosity, patience, and a willingness to learn, you're already miles ahead of most first-time authors.

Your Mindset Matters

Writing and publishing a book is exciting—but let's be honest, it can also be overwhelming. One day, you're buzzing with ideas, and words are flowing like a river. The next day, you're staring at a blinking cursor, wondering if anyone will ever want to read what you've written. That's normal. Every author, from first-timers to seasoned bestsellers, experiences highs and lows.

The difference between finishing a book and abandoning it often comes down to mindset.

Here are a few truths to keep in mind:

- **It won't be perfect—and that's okay.**
  First drafts are meant to be messy. Your job is to get the words down. You can fix them later.

- **Progress beats perfection.**
  Writing a page a day may not feel like much, but in a year you'll have a book-length manuscript. Small steps add up.
- **You'll make mistakes.**
  Formatting woes, typos, or awkward cover attempts—consider them part of the learning curve. Each one teaches you something that makes your next book easier.
- **Comparison is a trap.**
  It's tempting to measure yourself against authors who've already published ten books or hit bestseller lists. Remember, they started where you are now: with an idea and a blank page.

A Long-Term Perspective

Self-publishing isn't just about this one book. It's about learning a set of skills you can use again and again. Think of your first book as both a product *and* a practice round. Each book you publish will be better, smoother, and more professional than the last.

If you approach the process with curiosity—treating each step as an experiment—you'll not only publish a book, you'll enjoy the journey far more.

- **Quick Exercise:**

Write this sentence on a sticky note and keep it where you write:

"I am learning, and every step brings me closer to holding my book in my hands."

When motivation dips, read it. Sometimes a gentle reminder is all you need to keep going.

With your mindset in place, it's time to move from planning into action. In the next chapter, we'll explore **The Writing Process**—how to actually get words on the page, whether you're writing solo, using AI as a creative helper, or blending both approaches.

Chapter 2 - The Writing Process

Now that you've explored *why* you're writing and *who* you're writing for, it's time to tackle the heart of the matter: *how do you actually get the book written?*

This is where many aspiring authors stumble. The dream of being published is exciting—but sitting down to turn a blank page into 30,000 or 60,000 words can feel intimidating. The good news is, you don't have to do it all at once, and you don't have to do it alone.

Writers today have more tools at their disposal than ever before. Some prefer the traditional route: sitting at a desk every morning with a cup of tea and simply writing until the story takes shape. Others like to use modern aids—AI tools that help brainstorm, outline, or polish sentences. And then there are those who use a mixture of both, blending their creativity with AI's speed to make the process smoother.

Whatever approach you take, remember this: **there's no one "correct" way to write a book.** Some writers outline everything in detail before typing a word, while others dive in and discover the story as they go. Some write every day without fail; others work in bursts when inspiration strikes.

The important thing is to find the process that works for *you*. This chapter will walk you through three common approaches—writing on your own, using AI as an assistant, and using AI as a co-writer—along with strategies for overcoming that dreaded writer's block. By the end, you'll see that getting your first draft written is not only possible but far more manageable than it might seem right now.

Writing on Your Own: Building a Routine

At its core, writing a book still comes down to one thing: sitting down and getting words on the page. It sounds simple, but it's where most would-be authors give up. Life gets busy, the glow of the initial idea fades, and before you know it, weeks have passed without a single new sentence.

The trick is to build a routine that makes writing a habit rather than a once-in-a-while activity. Think of it like exercise—you don't need a marathon on day one, you just need regular movement to build stamina.

Here are some ways to make writing part of your everyday life:

- **Set a word goal.** Some authors aim for 500 words a day, others go for 1,000. If that feels daunting, even 200 words a day adds up. Over a year, that's more than 70,000 words—a full novel!
- **Schedule it.** Treat writing time like any other appointment. Block it into your calendar, and don't let it slide. Even 30 minutes a day can move your book forward.
- **Find your time of day.** Morning larks often do best before the rest of the world wakes up. Night owls might find their creative spark after dinner. Test both and notice when your brain feels sharpest.
- **Create a ritual.** Light a candle, make a cup of tea, or put on a favourite playlist. Repeating the same small action before writing helps signal to your brain, *"It's time to create."*
- **Track your progress.** A simple word-count chart, or crossing off days on a calendar, can give you a surprising boost of motivation. Watching the pages stack up is deeply satisfying.

Quick Exercise:
Open a fresh notebook page (or create a new document) and write down:

1. Your ideal writing time of day.
2. A realistic daily or weekly word goal.
3. One small ritual you'll use to start each writing session.

Stick this note somewhere visible. Small, steady habits will get your book finished far faster than bursts of frantic writing followed by long gaps.

First Draft Mindset

If there's one golden rule of writing, it's this: *first drafts are supposed to be messy.* Think of them as scaffolding—you're just building the structure so you have something to refine later.

The biggest mistake new writers make is editing as they go. You know the pattern: you write a sentence, then re-read it, tweak a word, delete it, re-type it, move the comma… and suddenly 30 minutes have passed and you've written one line. It feels productive, but it's really a trap. Constantly editing breaks your flow, and worse—it can make you doubt yourself.

When you write a first draft, give yourself permission to:

- **Write badly.** Awkward sentences, clichés, clunky descriptions—it doesn't matter. You'll fix it later.
- **Leave gaps.** Not sure what to name a minor character? Just type "(NAME HERE)" and keep going.
- **Skip ahead.** If Chapter 3 is stuck, jump to Chapter 5. You can stitch it all together afterwards.
- **Ignore spelling and grammar.** Red squiggly lines are the enemy of momentum. Those can be fixed in editing.

Think of your draft as raw clay. No sculptor expects the lump of clay on the wheel to look like the finished statue—it's simply the material they'll shape. Your words are the same. Get the clay on the wheel first.

A Trick for Letting Go

If you struggle to silence the inner editor, try this:

- Turn off spellcheck - so incredibly helpful!
- Write in "drafting mode"—literally label your file *"Ugly First Draft"*.
- Set a timer for 20 minutes and forbid yourself from deleting anything until it rings.

You'll be amazed at how much more freely the words come when you stop worrying about perfection.

Quick Exercise:
Write this affirmation on a sticky note:

"Done is better than perfect. I can't edit a blank page."

Stick it above your writing space. Read it before every session. Over time, you'll retrain your brain to embrace messy beginnings as a natural and necessary part of the process.

1. Brainstorming Ideas

Stuck on where to start? You can ask AI to list possible angles, themes, or scenes.

- **Nonfiction:** You're writing a self-help book on time management. You might ask AI:
  "What are 10 common struggles people face with managing their time?"
  The AI could list procrastination, distractions, poor planning, multitasking, etc.—a ready-made pool of ideas you can expand in your own words.
- **Fiction:** You're writing a fantasy novel. You could ask:
  "Give me five unique magical systems that haven't been overused in fantasy."
  The AI might suggest magic based on sound vibrations, memories, or constellations—sparks you can then develop into something fresh and original.

2. Outlining Chapters or Scenes

Some writers freeze at the thought of structuring their book. AI can help create a skeleton outline that you then flesh out.

- **Nonfiction:** You're drafting a beginner's guide to urban gardening. Prompt:
  "Give me a rough chapter outline for a beginner's guide to balcony gardening."
  AI might suggest topics like choosing containers, selecting

plants, soil basics, watering, pests, and harvesting. You then rework the order and add personal tips.
- **Fiction:** You're planning a mystery novel. Prompt: *"Suggest a 10-chapter outline for a cosy mystery set in a seaside village."*
AI could draft a sequence including the crime, red herrings, village gossip, hidden clues, and the final reveal. You then adapt this to fit your plot and characters.

3. Rephrasing Clunky Sentences

Sometimes you know what you want to say, but the words come out stiff or awkward. AI can offer smoother phrasing.

- **Nonfiction:**
Your draft: *"Writers often stop writing because they're too busy fixing things."*
AI suggestion: *"Many writers stall because they edit as they go, breaking their flow."*
You choose, combine, or tweak until it feels natural.
- **Fiction:**
Your draft: *"The castle was very big and had lots of rooms."*
AI suggestion: *"The sprawling castle loomed above, its endless corridors twisting into shadowy chambers."*
You can then tone it up or down depending on the mood you want.

4. Generating Prompts to Spark Creativity

AI can help kick-start your imagination.

- **Nonfiction:**
Prompt: *"Suggest five engaging ways to open a chapter about stress management for kids."*
AI might suggest scenarios like a child before a school test, a bedtime worry, or a sports competition. You pick the one that suits your audience and expand.
- **Fiction:**
Prompt: *"Give me three possible ways my detective could discover a hidden letter without it feeling cliché."*
AI might suggest finding it behind a painting, tucked inside

an old cookbook, or hidden in a piano bench. You then choose and shape the one that best fits your story.

Why Use AI This Way?

Because it saves time. Instead of staring at a blank page, you instantly have a handful of directions to choose from. You're still the driver—AI just helps map out the routes.

Quick Exercise:
Pick one spot in your book idea where you're stuck. Ask AI:

"Give me five different ways to approach [your topic/scene]."

Choose one suggestion and run with it. Even if you don't use it exactly, the fresh angle can get your creativity moving again.

Using AI as a Co-Writer

While many authors use AI as a light-touch assistant, others go further and let it generate whole paragraphs, sections, or even draft chapters. This can save a huge amount of time, especially for nonfiction, but it does come with responsibilities. AI text needs shaping, fact-checking, and personalisation. Left untouched, it can sound flat or generic.

The secret is to treat AI-generated text like a first draft created by an enthusiastic intern—you'll need to refine it to match your vision and voice.

Nonfiction Example

Let's say you're writing a self-help book on stress management. You ask AI:
"Write a short section explaining why daily journaling helps reduce stress."

AI might generate something like:

- *"Journaling allows people to release their thoughts and emotions onto paper, providing clarity and reducing feelings of overwhelm. It also creates a record of progress, helping individuals track patterns in their stress and develop healthier coping strategies."*

This is clear and useful—but it's also a bit bland. You can bring it to life by weaving in your own voice, anecdotes, and style:

- *"Think of a journal as a pressure valve for your mind. When worries swirl around, writing them down gets them out of your head and onto the page. You'll often spot patterns—like always feeling anxious before Monday meetings—that you can then tackle head-on. It's not about perfect sentences; it's about lightening the load."*

Result: The AI gave you the bones, but your rewrite gave it heart.

Fiction Example

Suppose you're writing a mystery novel. You ask AI:
"Describe a scene where the detective discovers a hidden letter in a library."

AI draft:

- *"The detective noticed a loose book on the shelf. Pulling it free, he found an envelope tucked behind it. Inside was a letter that revealed the truth about the missing heir."*

It's serviceable, but generic. Now, you take over:

- *"Inspector Peters ran a finger along the dusty spines until one book wobbled beneath his touch. Odd. He slid it free and a yellowed envelope fluttered to the floor. The paper was brittle, the ink smudged as though written in haste. His heart quickened. At last, a voice from the past was about to speak."*

Again, the AI gave you the skeleton, but you added atmosphere, detail, and tension.

Best Practices When Co-Writing With AI

Using AI as a co-writer can speed things up dramatically—but it also comes with responsibility. Think of it as hiring a very eager assistant who works fast but doesn't always know your style, your facts, or your audience. Your role is to direct, refine, and polish.

Here are some best practices to make sure the final product feels professional, personal, and authentically yours:

1. Edit Everything

- **Nonfiction:** AI can spit out neat summaries of topics, but sometimes they're overly formal or generic. Always run through the draft, simplifying or rewriting so it sounds like *you*.
- **Fiction:** AI can generate dialogue, but it might sound flat or out of character. Use it as a placeholder, then rewrite with the quirks, humour, or emotional beats that belong to your characters.

Rule of thumb: if you wouldn't say it out loud, rewrite it.

2. Fact-Check Relentlessly

- **Nonfiction:** AI sometimes invents statistics, misquotes experts, or confuses sources. Verify every claim with a reliable reference. If you're writing health, finance, or history, accuracy matters hugely to your credibility.
- **Fiction:** You don't need to fact-check magical spells or alien planets—but if your story mentions real places, time periods, or professions, make sure the details hold up. Readers will notice mistakes.

3. Add Personal Touches

- **Nonfiction:** Bring in your own anecdotes, stories, or case studies. AI can't replicate your lived experience—that's what makes your book unique.

- **Fiction:** Inject sensory details, emotions, and character backstory. AI might describe a forest, but only you know how your heroine *feels* walking through it.

Your voice + your perspective = the difference between a forgettable book and a memorable one.

4. Blend Styles
Don't treat AI output as a finished chapter. Think of it as scaffolding or a sketch. You're the painter who adds depth, colour, and texture.

- **Nonfiction:** Let AI list "10 benefits of meditation," then you explain which ones matter most, add a client's story, and guide the reader with your own insights.
- **Fiction:** Let AI suggest a chase scene, then you rewrite it with pacing, humour, or drama that fits your tone.

5. Keep Ethical Boundaries in Mind
Readers value authenticity. If AI played a role in drafting, that's fine—you don't need to hide it. But be clear with yourself that the final voice, creativity, and responsibility rest with you. Remember, *your readers are here for you, not a machine.*

Quick Exercise:
Take one AI-generated paragraph (fiction or nonfiction). Now:

1. Highlight anything bland, vague, or inaccurate.
2. Rewrite it with your personal voice, adding details only *you* could know.
3. Compare the two versions. Notice how much stronger, clearer, and more "you" the second one feels.

When It Works Best

AI isn't a magic wand that writes a bestseller while you sip tea. But it *is* a tool that can save you time, spark creativity, and help you push through roadblocks—if you use it in the right places. Here's where AI really comes into its own:

How to Self-Publish on a Budget

Nonfiction

- **Summarising information.** AI can quickly condense complex topics into bite-sized explanations. For example, in a health book you might ask it to explain how sleep affects stress, then you refine and add your perspective.
- **Drafting explanations.** Teaching something step-by-step? AI can create a simple framework (like "5 stages of habit change") that you then expand with examples and advice.
- **Generating lists and ideas.** Need 20 journaling prompts for stress relief? AI can draft them in seconds, saving you hours of brainstorming.
- **Providing structure.** If you're unsure how to order your material, AI can suggest a chapter outline or logical flow you can adjust to suit your goals.

Fiction

- **Scene sketching.** AI can quickly rough out a scene—say, a detective walking into a suspect's office—so you don't get stuck staring at a blank page. You then rewrite it with atmosphere, dialogue, and voice.
- **Brainstorming plot twists.** Stuck in the middle of your novel? Ask AI for five possible turns the story could take. You might reject most, but even one spark can unlock your next chapter.
- **World-building details.** Writing fantasy or sci-fi? AI can suggest cultural traditions, magical systems, or futuristic tech. You then refine them to suit your world.
- **Naming inspiration.** Need names for towns, minor characters, or pets? AI can generate lists that you cherry-pick from.

The Balance
The sweet spot is letting AI handle the *grunt work*—the lists, drafts, and raw material—while you handle the *soul of the book*: your voice, your stories, your perspective, your creativity.

Think of it like cooking with a meal-prep assistant: AI chops the onions, but you decide the recipe, add the spices, and serve the dish.

Quick Reflection:

Ask yourself: *"Which part of writing feels hardest for me—ideas, structure, or polishing?"*

That's where AI can help the most. Use it to ease your weak spots so you can focus on what you love: sharing your story.

Overcoming Writer's Block

Every writer hits a wall at some point. Maybe you sit down to write and nothing comes. Maybe you've started strong but now feel stuck in the middle. Or maybe the inner critic won't stop whispering, *"This isn't good enough."*

The important thing to remember is this: writer's block is not a sign you're a bad writer. It's a normal part of the process. The trick is learning how to loosen the knot and get the words flowing again.

1. Change the Scenery

Sometimes the quickest cure for a stuck brain is simply to move it somewhere new—fresh surroundings can trigger fresh ideas.

- **Nonfiction:** If you're stuck writing a chapter on productivity, try drafting bullet points at the library, or sketching a mind map in a café. A new setting can jolt your brain into gear.
- **Fiction:** Move your writing outdoors or to a new room. Sometimes shifting your environment helps you see the scene from a fresh angle.

2. Skip Ahead

Who says you have to write your book in order? If one section feels like pulling teeth, leapfrog to a part you're excited about and keep the momentum alive.

- **Nonfiction:** Don't know how to open Chapter 4? Jump to Chapter 6 and write the section you *do* feel excited about. Later, you can bridge the gap.
- **Fiction:** Stuck in the middle? Write the ending scene instead. Many novelists find that knowing where they're heading makes the middle easier to navigate.

3. Use Timed Writing Sprints

Set a timer for 15–20 minutes. Tell yourself you only need to write until it rings. Often, momentum takes over once you begin.

- **Nonfiction:** Use a sprint to dump raw notes for a section, without worrying about flow. You can organise later.
- **Fiction:** Write pure description or dialogue for 15 minutes, even if it's rough. The goal is movement, not perfection.

4. Ask "What's Stopping Me?"

Sometimes writer's block is really fear in disguise.

- Fear of not being good enough.
- Fear of wasting time.
- Fear of what others will think.

Naming the fear takes away its power. Write it down, acknowledge it, and then keep going anyway.

5. Use AI as a Jump-Starter

When you're staring at the page with no idea how to continue, AI can offer a quick spark.

- **Nonfiction prompt:** *"Give me five opening sentences for a chapter about managing stress before exams."*
- **Fiction prompt:** *"Suggest three ways my detective could realise the suspect is lying without saying 'he knew she lied.'"*

Even if you don't use the AI's wording, the ideas can nudge you forward.

6. Lower the Stakes

One of the sneakiest causes of writer's block is putting too much pressure on yourself. You sit down expecting brilliance, and when the words don't sparkle, you freeze. The truth is, no one writes a masterpiece in the first draft—not even bestselling authors.

Give yourself permission to write something ordinary, even clumsy. You can fix clumsiness later; you can't fix a blank page. Remind yourself: today's job is just to get words down, not to impress anyone. Tomorrow you can edit, polish, and refine.

Think of writing as sketching. Artists don't expect the first pencil lines to be perfect—they're the framework that makes the painting possible. Your words are the same.

Quick Exercise:
Next time you're blocked, try this:

1. Set a timer for 10 minutes.
2. Write *anything* related to your book—snippets of dialogue, a list of points, even questions you're asking yourself.
3. When the timer ends, stop. Congratulate yourself. You've written.

Chances are, once you've started, you'll want to keep going.

With strategies for keeping the words flowing, you now have the tools to build your first draft—whether it's rough, rambling, or full of gaps. Remember, that's exactly what a first draft should be. The hard part is getting the words down; the fun part comes next.

Once your draft is on the page, it's time to roll up your sleeves and start shaping it into something you'll be proud to share. That's where editing comes in. In the next chapter, we'll explore how to polish your manuscript—whether you're doing it yourself, using AI to tighten your prose, or calling in professional help to give your book that final sparkle.

Chapter 3 - Editing Your Manuscript

So, you've got a first draft—congratulations! That alone puts you ahead of the thousands of people who dream of writing a book but never get past chapter one. But here's the truth: your draft isn't ready for the world yet.

Editing is where the magic happens. It's where clunky sentences become smooth, ideas become clear, and your story or message takes its final shape. Think of writing as pouring clay onto the wheel—editing is where you sculpt it into something beautiful.

In this chapter, we'll look at the different levels of editing, DIY strategies, free and paid tools, and when it's worth calling in professional help.

Types of Editing

Editing isn't a single step you do once. It's more like peeling an onion—each layer gets you closer to the polished core. Understanding these layers will help you approach editing without overwhelm.

1. Developmental Editing (the big picture)
This is the "zoomed-out" stage. You're not worrying about commas—you're asking, *does this book work as a whole?*

- **Nonfiction:** Are the chapters in a logical order? Does each section build on the one before? If you're writing a guide, do readers move smoothly from problem to solution?
  Example: In a parenting book, you might realise you've explained bedtime strategies *after* your section on morning routines. Reordering chapters makes the advice clearer.
- **Fiction:** Do the plot, pacing, and character arcs make sense? Are there holes in the story? Does the ending satisfy the promise set up at the beginning?
  Example: In your mystery novel, you might find your big

reveal happens too suddenly, without enough clues earlier. This happened to me as I read through the draft and consequently developed a slightly different scenario adding in a red herring. Developmental editing means going back and planting those hints.

2. Line Editing (sentence-level flow)

This stage is about style, tone, and readability. You're polishing sentences so they're engaging and smooth. It is also the stage where reading aloud really shines. (see below)

Examples of Line-edits:

- **Nonfiction:** Are you speaking directly to your audience, or slipping into academic jargon?
  Example: Original: *"Stress may be alleviated through the utilisation of diaphragmatic breathing techniques."*
  Line edit: *"Stress eases when you take a few slow, deep breaths into your belly."*
- **Fiction:** Do your sentences carry rhythm? Is the dialogue natural?
  Example: Original: *"He walked quickly down the dark street, feeling nervous."*
  Line edit: *"He hurried along the dark street, every shadow tugging at his nerves."*

Read Aloud Checklist

Reading your manuscript out loud is one of the cheapest and most effective editing tools you'll ever use. When you hear your sentences spoken, you can instantly tell if they're clunky, too long, or lack rhythm. Dialogue also jumps out as either natural or stiff.

Here's how to get the most out of it:

Choose the right stage

- Best during **line editing** (to check style and flow).
- Useful again in **copyediting/proofreading** for accuracy.

Read slowly and clearly
Don't skim. Speak each word as written—you'll notice missing words, awkward phrasing, or repetitions that your eyes gloss over.

Listen for rhythm
Does the sentence flow naturally? Or do you run out of breath halfway through? Long, clunky sentences become obvious when spoken.

Check dialogue (for fiction)
Does it sound like something a real person would say? If it feels stiff or robotic when spoken aloud, it'll feel that way to readers too.

Check tone (for nonfiction)
Does your voice sound approachable and clear? If you stumble over jargon or complex words, your reader probably will too.

Mark, don't fix immediately
Keep a pencil handy. When you spot an issue, mark it and keep reading. Fixing as you go breaks your rhythm (and can trigger that inner editor).

Optional: Use text-to-speech
Hearing your book read back in a computer voice highlights typos and repeated words you may still miss.

- **Quick Exercise:**

Take one page of your manuscript and read it aloud. Circle every spot where you stumble, run out of breath, or think, *"I'd never say it that way."* Rewrite those sections so they flow as smoothly out loud as they do on the page.

3. Copyediting (technical precision)
Now it's time for the nuts and bolts: grammar, spelling, punctuation, and consistency.

- **Nonfiction:** Are you using US or UK spelling? Is "Chapter 3" titled in the same style as "Chapter 7"?
  Example: Switching between "organisation" and

"organization" makes a book look sloppy. Copyediting fixes that.
- **Fiction:** Are character names spelled consistently? Does the date on page 12 match the timeline on page 50?
Example: Your heroine is "Katherine" in Chapter 1 but "Kathryn" in Chapter 5. A copyeditor catches this.

4. Proofreading (final polish)
This is the very last step before publishing. Proofreading catches the small mistakes that slip through even after multiple edits.

- **Nonfiction:** Typos in headers, missing page numbers, or a misplaced decimal in a figure.
Example: Writing "$10,00" instead of "$10,000."
- **Fiction:** Missing quotation marks, an extra "the," or a misspelled word.
Example: "He ran into to the room" instead of "He ran into the room."

- **Quick Tip:**

Don't try to do all four types at once—it's exhausting and ineffective. Work from the big picture (developmental) down to the fine detail (proofreading). It's like building a house: frame the structure first, then decorate the walls, then polish the trim.

DIY Self-Editing

Your first round of editing is best done by you. No one knows your story, message, or audience better than you do. In fact, self-editing is one of the most empowering parts of the publishing journey.

Why? Because it saves you time, money, and stress. A messy, unedited draft handed to a professional editor can cost more (and take longer to fix). But if you tidy it yourself first, the editor can focus on higher-level improvements rather than correcting every typo or repeated word. Even if you never hire an editor, self-editing ensures your book feels polished and professional.

The DIY method also gives you a deeper understanding of your own writing habits. You'll start to notice patterns: maybe you overuse certain words, slip into passive voice, or write dialogue that's too formal. Catching these quirks now will make your future books stronger.

And here's the real benefit: you'll learn to trust your own voice. By shaping your draft through several self-editing passes, you gain confidence that your words can hold their own on the page. The process isn't just about fixing mistakes—it's about discovering the best version of your book.

Here is a step-by-step process to follow:

Step 1: Take a Break

- Put the manuscript away for at least a week. Fresh eyes will spot things you completely missed when you were too close to the words.
- *Fiction example:* After a pause, you may notice your pacing drags in the middle chapters.
- *Nonfiction example:* A section that once felt clear now reads as confusing or repetitive.

Step 2: Read Through Without Editing

- Do a "reader's pass." Read straight through without changing anything, just noticing where you stumble, skim, or lose interest.
- Jot notes in the margin: *"too long," "unclear,"* or *"great, keep this."*

Step 3: Big Picture Fixes (Developmental)

- Rearrange or cut chapters if needed.
- *Fiction:* Does every scene move the story forward? If not, cut or combine.
- *Nonfiction:* Are you repeating the same advice in different chapters? Can you streamline?

Step 4: Chapter-by-Chapter Checks (Line Editing)

- Work through each chapter slowly.
- *Fiction:* Does dialogue sound natural? Are character voices distinct?
- *Nonfiction:* Does each chapter deliver on its promise? Is the language clear for your intended reader?

Step 5: Trim the Filler

- Cut unnecessary words like "just," "really," "very," and "that."
- *Example:* "She just really wanted to leave" → "She wanted to leave."

Step 6: Consistency Pass

- *Fiction:* Check timelines, character details, locations. Did your heroine's hair colour change halfway through? You may discover your hero's eyes are blue in Chapter 2 and brown in Chapter 8. Readers will catch it!
- *Nonfiction:* Check terminology. Did you use "time blocking" in one section and "calendar batching" in another? Choose one term and stick with it. In a chapter about nutrition, you might notice you used "processed food" in one section and "junk food" in another—pick one and stick with it.

Step 7: Read Aloud

- Use the **Read Aloud Checklist** from earlier.
- You'll catch clunky sentences, typos, and dialogue issues much faster this way.

Step 8: Polishing (Copyediting Basics)

- Run the manuscript through a tool like Grammarly, ProWritingAid, or Hemingway to catch grammar, style, and clarity issues.
- Don't blindly accept every suggestion—trust your voice.

Step 9: Final Sweep (Proofreading Basics)
This is the polishing stage—the last chance to catch small errors before publishing. Go slowly and check carefully.

Here's what to look for:

- **Typos and misspellings.** The tiny mistakes your eyes skim past.
- **Punctuation errors.** Missing quotation marks, extra commas, or misplaced apostrophes.
- **Formatting consistency.** Check fonts, line spacing, and paragraph alignment.
- **Chapter headings and numbers.** Make sure they're numbered correctly and match the table of contents.
- **Page breaks.** Each new chapter should start cleanly on its own page.
- **Widows and orphans.** (Single words or lines stranded at the top or bottom of a page—can look messy in print.)
- **Italics and bold.** Are they used consistently (e.g., book titles italicised, emphasis in bold)?
- **Table of contents.** Do page numbers match the actual chapters? (Nonfiction especially!)
- **Figures, charts, or images.** Make sure captions are correct and everything is in the right place.
- **The ending.** Proofread your last few pages carefully—typos love to hide there because by then, you're tired.

- **Quick Exercise:**

Choose one chapter of your draft and run it through this 9-step process. Notice how much stronger, clearer, and tighter it feels—even before professional editing.
Also:
If possible, proofread in a different format than you wrote in. For

example, export your manuscript as a PDF or print it out. Mistakes often pop out more clearly in a new layout.

NOTE: *At the end of this book, I've given you a mini checklist. If you can, take a copy, print it out, and have it on your desk.*

Free and Low-Cost Tools

You don't need an expensive editing package to polish your manuscript. Several free or budget-friendly tools can help catch errors, smooth sentences, and tighten your writing. Think of these as digital helpers—not replacements for your judgment, but useful extra eyes.

1. Grammarly (Free & Paid)

- **Pros:** Easy to use, catches grammar, spelling, and punctuation errors, integrates with Word and Google Docs.
- **Cons:** The free version is limited; the paid version can be a bit pricey. Sometimes it makes suggestions that flatten your style.
- **Best for nonfiction:** Spotting typos, grammar slips, and over-complicated sentences in business or self-help books.
- **Best for fiction:** Useful for catching missing words or punctuation, but beware—its "fixes" can strip personality from dialogue.

2. ProWritingAid (Free trial & Paid)

- **Pros:** Excellent for deeper analysis—flags overused words, pacing issues, sentence variety, and sticky sentences.
- **Cons:** The free version is limited to 500 words at a time. Full access requires a subscription.
- **Best for nonfiction:** Great for improving clarity and avoiding repetition in instructional or academic-style writing.

- **Best for fiction:** Fantastic for spotting clichés, overly long sentences, and areas where pacing drags.

3. Hemingway App (Free online & Paid desktop)

- **Pros:** Highlights hard-to-read sentences, passive voice, and adverbs. Colour-coded for simplicity.
- **Cons:** Can be blunt—sometimes too harsh on creative prose. Doesn't check grammar.
- **Best for nonfiction:** Brilliant for simplifying dense topics and ensuring your writing is reader-friendly.
- **Best for fiction:** Good for trimming long descriptive passages, but be careful not to lose your style—sometimes a complex sentence adds mood.

4. AI Editing Tools (ChatGPT, Claude, etc.)

- **Pros:** Can rephrase awkward passages, explain concepts in simpler language, or suggest variations of a sentence.
- **Cons:** May "over-polish" and make writing sound generic. Must always be reviewed and adapted by you.
- **Best for nonfiction:** Helpful for rewording clunky explanations or summarising research.
- **Best for fiction:** Great for brainstorming alternative phrasings for dialogue or descriptions—but always rewrite to keep your unique voice.

5. Built-in Spellcheck (Word, Google Docs, etc.)

- **Pros:** Free, simple, always there.
- **Cons:** Limited to basic spelling/grammar. Won't catch context errors (e.g., "their" vs. "there").
- **Best for nonfiction & fiction:** A quick first sweep before moving to deeper editing tools.

Tip: Try using two tools in combination. For example, run your text through Grammarly for grammar, then Hemingway for readability. Together, they give you a clearer picture of where your writing can improve.

⚠ *But remember: tools are assistants, not replacements. They can highlight issues, but you decide whether to change them.*

Once you've done your DIY passes with tools, you'll already be miles ahead of most first-time authors. Your manuscript will be cleaner, sharper, and easier to read—which means if you decide to hire an editor, their job will be faster and often cheaper (since they won't be fixing basic errors). Even if you don't bring in outside help, these tools will give your book a more professional polish and help you feel confident it's ready for the next stage.

But there's a limit to what software can do. Tools can catch grammar slips and highlight clunky sentences, but they can't always judge flow, emotional impact, or whether your book actually works for your intended audience. That's where professional editors—or at least thoughtful feedback from other humans—can make all the difference.

In the next section, we'll explore **when and how to bring in an editor**, what kinds of editing services exist, how much they cost, and what to expect from the process.

Bringing in an Editor

Even the best writers benefit from another pair of eyes. After all, when you've been living inside your manuscript for weeks or months, it's easy to miss gaps, typos, or clunky passages. A professional editor can bring clarity, polish, and perspective that you simply can't achieve alone.

That said, editors can be expensive, so it's worth understanding what types of editing they offer, where to find them, and how to choose the right one for your book.

Types of Editors

Different editors specialise in different stages of the process:

- **Developmental Editor**
  Focuses on structure, big-picture flow, and content.

- *Nonfiction:* They'll check if your chapters are in the right order, if your argument builds logically, and if anything important is missing.
- *Fiction:* They'll flag plot holes, weak character development, or pacing issues.
- **Line Editor**
Works at the sentence level to improve readability and style.
  - *Nonfiction:* Helps you sound clear, engaging, and consistent.
  - *Fiction:* Polishes descriptions, smooths dialogue, and ensures your prose flows.
- **Copyeditor**
Catches grammar, punctuation, spelling, and consistency issues.
  - Both fiction and nonfiction benefit here—especially with details like UK vs US spelling, capitalisation, and fact-checking.
- **Proofreader**
The final polish. They catch stray typos, formatting issues, and last-minute errors before publishing.

Tip: If budget is tight, focus on copyediting and proofreading. These ensure your book looks professional and avoids distracting mistakes.

Where to Find Editors

- **Reedsy:** A curated marketplace of professional editors (higher quality, higher cost).
- **Fiverr / Upwork:** Wide range of editors at varying prices—be sure to check reviews carefully.
- **Writing groups / local networks:** Some editors work freelance within writing communities—often more affordable.
- **Beta readers:** Not professional editors, but experienced readers who give feedback on clarity, flow, and engagement. Free or low-cost.

How to Choose the Right Editor

1. **Decide what level you need.** Big-picture help? Style polish? Or just a last typo check?
2. **Ask for a sample edit.** Most professional editors will do a free or low-cost sample on 1,000 words. This shows you their style before committing.
3. **Check reviews and experience.** Do they specialise in your genre? A fantasy editor may not be the best choice for a medical guide.
4. **Be clear on expectations.** Agree on deadlines, cost, and what's included before you begin.

Costs (Approximate Ranges)

Note: Prices vary by editor experience and genre. These examples are only ballpark figures to help you budget.

- **Developmental Editing**: $0.03–$0.08 per word
  - 50,000 words × $0.03 = **$1,500**
  - 50,000 words × $0.08 = **$4,000**
- **Line Editing**: $0.02–$0.05 per word
  - 50,000 words × $0.02 = **$1,000**
  - 50,000 words × $0.05 = **$2,500**
- **Copyediting**: $0.01–$0.03 per word
  - 50,000 words × $0.01 = **$500**
  - 50,000 words × $0.03 = **$1,500**
- **Proofreading**: $0.005–$0.01 per word
  - 50,000 words × $0.005 = **$250**
  - 50,000 words × $0.01 = **$500**

At a glance:

- A full edit from start to finish (developmental + line + copyedit + proofread) could cost anywhere from **$3,250** on the low end to **$8,500+** on the high end for a 50,000-word book.

- Many first-time authors compromise by focusing on **copyediting + proofreading** only, which keeps costs between **$750–$2,000**, depending on the editor.

Note: Prices can be lower on sites like Fiverr, but quality varies.

Budgeting Tips for Editing on a Shoestring

Editing can be one of the biggest expenses in self-publishing, but there are ways to keep costs manageable without sacrificing quality.

1. Do multiple DIY passes first.
The cleaner your manuscript, the less work (and cost) for any editor you hire. Use tools like Grammarly or Hemingway, and follow the DIY editing steps earlier in this chapter.

2. Use beta readers.
Find a handful of trusted readers—ideally people who enjoy your genre—and ask for honest feedback. They'll catch confusing sections, clunky dialogue, or missing explanations.

3. Swap edits with other writers.
Join writing groups or online forums where you can exchange manuscripts. A fresh pair of eyes from another writer is invaluable—and free.

4. Ask for a sample edit.
Before committing to an editor, request a 1,000-word sample. This shows you their style and helps you decide if the investment is worth it.

5. Prioritise proofing if money is tight.
If you can only afford one type of editing, go for **proofreading**. Readers forgive the occasional clunky sentence, but nothing ruins professionalism faster than typos.

6. Break projects into chunks.
Some editors allow you to hire them chapter by chapter. This can spread out costs and give you time to apply their feedback yourself to the rest of the manuscript.

7. Consider text-to-speech tools.
Listening to your book read aloud by software is a free way to catch errors your eyes miss.

With these strategies, even authors on a shoestring budget can polish their work to a professional standard.

Quick Exercise:
Write down which level of editing your book most needs right now (developmental, line, copy, or proof). Then list two possible options: one professional route (e.g., Reedsy editor) and one budget-friendly route (e.g., beta reader).

Editing with AI

AI can also help in the editing stage.

- **Nonfiction example:** Paste in a paragraph that feels clunky and ask AI to suggest simpler wording. Then choose or tweak the version that fits your style.
- **Fiction example:** If a scene feels flat, ask AI to "add more sensory detail." You'll get suggestions you can adapt, while keeping your voice intact.

The key, as always, is control—you're the editor-in-chief, not the AI.

Quick Exercise:
Take one page of your draft and try these three passes:

1. Read it aloud—mark anything that sounds awkward.
2. Run it through a tool like Hemingway—see if your sentences are too long.
3. Ask a trusted friend (or AI) to read it—note what they find confusing or dull.

You'll be surprised how much tighter your writing becomes after even one page of layered editing.

Chapter 4 - Formatting and Layout

Your manuscript is edited, polished, and full of potential. Now comes the part that turns it from a rough file into a *real book*: formatting. This is where the words you've worked so hard on are dressed up for the reader—whether that's someone flicking through a Kindle on the train or holding a paperback in their hands.

Formatting is often overlooked by beginners, but it makes a huge difference. A book with odd spacing, inconsistent fonts, or messy chapter headings looks unprofessional and can put readers off—even if the content is brilliant. On the other hand, a clean, well-formatted book disappears into the background, letting your words take centre stage.

The best news? You don't need to spend a fortune. With free or low-cost tools—and a little patience—you can format your book yourself. Many successful indie authors do exactly that in their early publishing journey. It's how I began, and how I still work today. Doing it myself not only saved money, it also gave me a deeper understanding of how publishing really works. In this chapter, we'll look at:

- Why formatting matters so much.
- How to prepare your book for e-readers like Kindle and Kobo.
- What to consider for print editions, including margins and page layout.
- The most popular (and budget-friendly) tools for formatting.
- When it's worth doing it yourself and when outsourcing might save time.

By the end, you'll know how to give your book the professional polish it deserves—without blowing your budget.

Why Formatting Matters

- **Professionalism:** Readers may forgive the odd typo, but a badly formatted book screams "self-published" in the worst way.
- **Readability:** Proper fonts, spacing, and layout make your book easy to read on any device.
- **Compatibility:** Different platforms (Kindle, Kobo, Apple Books, print-on-demand) have their own requirements. Good formatting ensures your book looks right everywhere.

Formatting for eBooks

EBooks are the easiest and most affordable way to get your work into readers' hands. They're portable, instant to download, and accessible on everything from Kindles to phones. But while digital publishing removes the cost of printing, it does add a few quirks. What looks fine in Word may look completely different on an e-reader. That's why proper formatting is essential.

The golden rule for eBooks is **keep it simple.** E-readers don't like fancy fonts, complex layouts, or heavy graphics. What you want is clean, consistent text that looks professional on any device.

Start with Styles

If you're using Word or Google Docs, apply built-in styles:

- **Heading 1** for chapter titles
- **Normal** for body text
- **Heading 2** (optional) for subheadings in nonfiction

This creates a logical structure in your file. When you convert it to Kindle or EPUB, the e-reader recognises those headings and builds a clickable table of contents.

Personal note: I still use Word for my first layout. It's straightforward, and once you get the hang of styles, it saves hours of frustration later.

Spacing and Paragraphs

- Use **single line spacing** for body text.
- Indent the first line of each paragraph (except the first one after a heading).
- Avoid hitting the space bar or Enter key repeatedly to "make it look right"—this causes chaos in eBook conversions.

Fiction example: Clear indents make dialogue easy to follow.
Nonfiction example: Bullet points and numbered lists help readers absorb information quickly.

Fonts and Size

Stick to standard fonts (Times New Roman, Georgia, or Arial). Readers can change font size on their device, so don't stress about making it "perfect" on your screen.

Images in eBooks

If you're adding images (common in nonfiction), keep them small and simple. High-resolution photos increase file size, which can raise delivery costs on Amazon. Aim for 300dpi images resized for digital.

Nonfiction example: Charts, diagrams, or step-by-step photos.
Fiction example: A small map at the beginning of a fantasy novel.

Preview Before Publishing

Never assume your file will display perfectly. Use Amazon's free **Kindle Previewer** to check how your book looks on different devices (Kindle Paperwhite, Fire tablet, phone app). This is where you'll catch odd breaks, missing indents, or images that don't sit right.

Tools That Help

- **Kindle Create (Free):** Amazon's own tool, very user-friendly for beginners.

- **Calibre (Free):** Great for converting to different eBook formats (EPUB, MOBI).
- **Atticus (Paid):** More advanced, works for both eBook and print formatting in one place.

Budget hack: Start with Kindle Create—it's free and produces a file Amazon will happily accept. Once you're more confident, you can try other tools.

Once your eBook looks good, you can shift focus to formatting for print—a little trickier, but still manageable with patience.

Formatting for Print (Paperback/Hardcover)

There's something magical about holding a printed copy of your book. An eBook is practical, but a paperback feels *real*—you can smell the pages, scribble notes in the margin, or proudly place it on your bookshelf. Luckily, print-on-demand services like Amazon KDP and IngramSpark make it possible to publish in print without huge upfront costs.

That said, print formatting is a little more fiddly than eBooks. Pages must look neat and balanced, margins need to be exact, and the file has to meet the printer's technical requirements. But don't worry—with the right steps, you can do this yourself.

1. Choose a Trim Size

This is the physical size of your book. Common choices are:

- **5" × 8"** – Popular for fiction (novels, memoirs).
- **6" × 9"** – Common for nonfiction, especially guides and reference books.
- **8.5" × 11"** – Best for workbooks, cookbooks, or anything with lots of images/diagrams.

Tip: Look at books in your genre and match their size—it helps your book "fit in" with reader expectations.

2. Set Margins and Gutters

- **Margins** are the blank space around text. Too small and the book looks cramped, too big and it feels sparse.
- **Gutter margin** is the extra space near the spine so text doesn't disappear when the book is bound.

Amazon KDP and IngramSpark both provide free templates with the correct margins based on your trim size and page count. Always start with one of these—trust me, it saves a lot of headaches.

3. Page Layout Basics

- **Paragraphs:** Use indents (not tabs or spaces).
- **Line spacing:** Usually 1.15–1.5 for readability.
- **Alignment:** Justified text looks neat in print.
- **Chapters:** Start each on a new page (ideally a right-hand page).

Fiction example: Chapters often begin halfway down the page, with the title centred.
Nonfiction example: Headings, subheadings, and bullet points should be clear and consistent.

4. Headers, Footers, and Page Numbers

- **Odd numbers** (1, 3, 5…) go on right-hand pages.
- **Even numbers** (2, 4, 6…) go on left-hand pages.
- **Headers:** Typically include author name on one side, book title on the other. Leave headers off chapter-opening pages.
- **Page numbers:** Bottom centre or outer corners are standard.

5. Watch Out for Widows and Orphans

In publishing, a **widow** is a single word stranded on its own line at the end of a paragraph. An **orphan** is the first line of a paragraph stuck at the bottom of a page. Both look messy. Most formatting software can prevent these automatically.

6. Images and Graphics

If your book includes pictures, charts, or illustrations:

- Use **300dpi resolution** for sharp print quality.
- Save in **black-and-white** if publishing a standard paperback (colour printing is far more expensive).
- Check that images sit within the margins and don't bleed off the page unless you've set up a bleed file.

Fiction example: A map or family tree at the start of the book.
Nonfiction example: Diagrams, charts, or checklists inside the chapters.

7. Export to PDF

Most print-on-demand services require a print-ready PDF. Export your Word, Google Docs, or Atticus/Vellum file as a PDF, making sure fonts are embedded and margins preserved. Always preview the PDF before uploading.

8. Test with a Proof Copy

Never skip this step! Order a proof copy before going live. Holding the physical book will reveal issues (margins too tight, text too small, headers misplaced) that you might miss on screen.

Personal aside: I always order a proof for every book. Even when I think I've set it up correctly, there's always something I want to tweak after seeing it in print.

Budget-Friendly Formatting Options

- **Kindle Create (Free):** Also works for print, not just Kindle eBooks.
- **Word or Google Docs (Free):** Use KDP templates for margins and gutters.

- **Atticus (Paid):** One-time cost, handles both eBook and print in one place.
- **Professional formatter:** $100–$500+ depending on complexity (worth it for heavily illustrated books).

Tools for Formatting

- **Microsoft Word / Google Docs** (Free if you already have them): Perfectly fine for DIY if you use styles correctly.
- **Calibre (Free):** Good for converting files into ePub or MOBI formats.
- **Kindle Create (Free):** Amazon's own tool—user-friendly and great for beginners.
- **Atticus (Paid, one-time):** Easy-to-use formatting software for both eBooks and print, cheaper than Vellum.
- **Vellum (Paid, Mac only):** Loved by many indie authors for its beautiful, professional layouts—but pricey.

DIY vs Outsourcing

- **DIY:** Costs little to nothing. Perfect if you're tech-comfortable and patient.
- **Outsource:** Costs range from $100–$500+ for a professional formatter. Worth considering if your book has lots of images, tables, or complex layouts (e.g., cookbooks).

With your print file prepared and a proof copy in hand, you're one step closer to holding a professional-quality book that feels just as polished as anything from a traditional publisher. Formatting may feel intimidating at first, but once you've done it once, it becomes much easier—and even a little addictive. There's nothing quite like flipping through the pages of a book you created yourself, spotting your name on the spine, and knowing it looks every bit as good as the titles on a bookstore shelf.

Next, we'll move into the practical (and sometimes confusing) world of **ISBNs and Metadata**—those little numbers and details that make your book "official," trackable, and discoverable in online stores and libraries.

Chapter 5 - ISBNs and Book Metadata

Every published book needs an "identity card." In the publishing world, that ID comes in the form of an ISBN and a bundle of details called metadata. These might sound technical—or even a little boring—but they're absolutely essential. Together, they tell bookstores, libraries, and online retailers exactly what your book is, how it should be listed, and how readers can find it.

Without them, your book risks getting lost in the sea of millions of titles already out there. With them, your book becomes official, trackable, and discoverable. Best of all, sorting out ISBNs and metadata isn't nearly as complicated as it first appears, and you can do much of it yourself on a shoestring budget.

What is an ISBN?

An **ISBN** (International Standard Book Number) is a unique 13-digit code that identifies a specific edition of a book. Think of it as your book's fingerprint.

- **EBooks, paperbacks, and audiobooks each need their own ISBN.**
    - One ISBN for your Kindle edition.
    - A different ISBN for your paperback.
    - Another ISBN again if you release it as an audiobook.
- If you change your book significantly (new edition, new title, major rewrite), you'll need a new ISBN.

Small updates (fixing typos, minor formatting changes) don't require a new ISBN.

Do You Need an ISBN?

- **For eBooks on Amazon KDP:** Technically, no. Amazon gives your eBook a free ASIN (Amazon Standard Identification Number), which works fine within their system.
- **For print books:** Yes. Amazon offers a free ISBN for paperbacks, but it will list them as the "publisher." If you buy your own, you can be listed as the publisher.

If you're budget-conscious and only publishing through Amazon, the free ISBN is enough. If you plan to distribute widely (e.g., through IngramSpark or to libraries), owning your ISBNs gives you more control.

Where Do You Get an ISBN?

- **Amazon KDP (Free):** Assigns one automatically for your paperback.
- **Bowker (US):** The official ISBN agency in the US (purchasing required).
- **Nielsen (UK):** The official ISBN agency for the UK.
- **Other countries:** Each has its own agency (often searchable online).
- **Cost:** In the US, a single ISBN from Bowker is about $125, but buying a block of 10 or more brings the cost per ISBN down. In the UK, Nielsen sells them in batches rather than individually. Some countries even offer ISBNs free of charge. For example, in New Zealand (where I live), they are free—but there's a catch. Once the book is published, I'm required to send a copy in the same format as the ISBN (print, eBook, etc.) to the National Library for legal deposit. It's a fair exchange, and it means my books are preserved in the country's official collection.

Free ISBN vs Own ISBN: Pros and Cons

Option	Pros	Cons	Best For
Free ISBN (from Amazon KDP or other platforms)	- No cost (great for beginners on a budget). - Instantly assigned by the platform. - No paperwork involved.	- Lists the platform (e.g. Amazon) as the "publisher," not you. - Usually can't be used outside that platform (limits distribution). - If you later want to switch platforms, you'll need a new ISBN.*	Authors starting out, publishing only on Amazon, or testing the waters with self-publishing.
Own ISBN (purchased from Bowker, Nielsen, or your country's agency)	- You are listed as the official publisher (looks more professional). - You can use the same ISBN across multiple platforms (Amazon, IngramSpark, Kobo, etc.) for that format. - More control over your publishing rights and brand.	- Costly in some countries (e.g. $125 per ISBN in the US). - Requires more admin (registering and assigning ISBNs). - Each format/version of your book needs its own ISBN.	Authors planning wide distribution, building a long-term author brand, or publishing multiple books.

*NOTE:

- If you publish a **print book** on Amazon KDP and use their **free ISBN**, Amazon will list *themselves* as the publisher of

that edition. That ISBN is tied to Amazon's system. If later you want to distribute the same print book through another platform (like IngramSpark), you **cannot reuse Amazon's free ISBN**. You'd need to assign a **new ISBN that you own** for the IngramSpark edition.
- For **eBooks**, Amazon doesn't require an ISBN at all. They use their own identifier called an **ASIN** (Amazon Standard Identification Number). If you want to publish the eBook elsewhere (Apple, Kobo, etc.), you can either:
    o Publish it without an ISBN (most platforms accept that), or
    o Assign your own ISBN for consistency across platforms.

So the simple rule is:

- Free ISBN = tied to that platform only.
- Owned ISBN = portable across platforms.

In practice, many indie authors start with free ISBNs to test the waters, then move to their own once they're ready to publish more widely or build a professional imprint.

What is Metadata?

Metadata is the information about your book that helps readers (and online stores) find it. It's just as important as your cover. Done well, it makes your book discoverable; done poorly, it leaves your book invisible.

Metadata includes:

- **Title and subtitle**
- **Author name**
- **Series title** (if applicable)
- **Description/blurb**
- **Keywords** (the search terms readers might type into Amazon)

- **Categories/genres** (where your book sits on the virtual shelf)

Fiction Metadata Example

- Title: *The Forgotten Heir*
- Subtitle: *A Victorian Mystery*
- Author: Jane Smith
- Categories: Historical mystery, Women sleuths
- Keywords: "Victorian detective," "mystery series," "female sleuth"

Nonfiction Metadata Example

- Title: *Stress Management for Kids*
- Subtitle: *A Parent's Guide to Understanding Triggers, Reducing Anxiety, and Raising Resilient Children*
- Author: Fee O'Shea
- Categories: Parenting, Child Psychology
- Keywords: "stress management for children," "helping kids with anxiety," "resilient parenting"

Why Metadata Matters

Think of metadata as your book's shop window. If your categories and keywords don't match what readers are searching for, your book won't appear in results—even if it's exactly what they want.

- **Good metadata:** Targets the right readers, boosts discoverability, and helps your book climb charts in smaller categories.
- **Bad metadata:** Buries your book under millions of others, no matter how good the content is.

Quick Exercise:
Open Amazon and search for books in your genre. Note the categories, subtitles, and keywords in the top-selling books. Write down 5–10 keywords or phrases that you could apply to your own book.

With your ISBNs and metadata sorted, your book is now both official and discoverable. Think of it as giving your book a passport and address—without them, it can't travel far or be found easily. The next step, however, is just as important: how your book *looks*. Readers really do judge a book by its cover, and a strong design can be the difference between someone clicking "buy" or scrolling past.

In the next chapter, we'll dive into **cover design**—why it matters, the DIY tools you can use on a budget, and how to create a cover that not only looks professional but also speaks directly to your ideal reader.

Chapter 6 - Cover Design

You've polished your words and given your book its "passport" with an ISBN. Now comes the part that most readers will notice first—your cover.

It may not feel fair, but it's true: people really do judge a book by its cover. In fact, the cover is often your single most powerful marketing tool. Before anyone reads your description or your carefully crafted opening chapter, they'll glance at the cover and make an instant decision: *Does this look like the kind of book I want to read?*

A great cover does two things:

1. **Catches attention.** It stands out in a crowded online store or on a physical shelf.
2. **Sets expectations.** It tells readers the genre, tone, and style of the book at a glance. A thriller cover looks very different from a cosy romance. A self-help guide should signal clarity and authority, not confusion.

The best part? You don't have to spend a fortune to create a professional-looking cover. With free and low-cost tools available today, even first-time authors on a tight budget can produce a design that looks polished and sells.

Why Covers Matter

Your cover is the very first impression your book makes. Long before a potential reader sees your beautifully written blurb or your carefully chosen keywords, they see the cover—and in that split second, they decide whether to take a closer look or keep scrolling.

Think of your cover as your book's shop window. If the display is inviting, people will step inside. If it looks confusing or unprofessional, they'll pass by—even if the content inside is brilliant.

A good cover does three key things:

1. **Grabs attention.** It pops out from a crowded page of thumbnails on Amazon or a physical bookshelf.
2. **Signals genre.** A crime thriller, a cosy romance, and a children's book all need very different visual cues. Readers expect certain styles, and if your cover doesn't match, they may not realise your book is for them.
3. **Builds trust.** A professional-looking cover reassures readers that the writing inside is also worth their time.

Examples of Strong vs Weak Covers

- *Fiction:* A well-designed mystery novel might feature a moody landscape, bold typography, and muted colours that hint at suspense. A weak one might use clip-art magnifying glasses and Comic Sans font—readers instantly sense it's amateurish.
- *Nonfiction:* A strong self-help guide will have clean fonts, clear colour contrasts, and maybe a symbolic image (like a ladder or a sunrise). A weak one may cram too many images on the page or use busy fonts that look messy at thumbnail size.

Enjoying the Creative Process

Designing your cover can actually be one of the most fun parts of publishing—this is where you get to let your imagination run.

Here are some DIY-friendly ways to play with ideas:

- **Ask AI for concepts.** AI image tools can generate unique visuals based on your prompts (e.g., "vintage-style mystery cover with a manor house in the background"). Even if you don't use them directly, they're great for sparking ideas.
- **Use Canva templates.** Canva has ready-made book cover layouts where you can swap fonts, colours, and images. It's budget-friendly, intuitive, and produces professional-looking results.
- **Create multiple drafts.** Don't stop at one design—mock up three or four covers.

- **Test with your audience.** Share your drafts on social media or with friends and ask, *"Which cover makes you want to pick up the book?"* It's a fun way to involve your readers and get honest feedback.

Personal aside: This is one of the parts I really enjoy. Playing with layouts, colours, and fonts is a chance to be creative in a whole different way. I've often asked my social media friends to vote on their favourite draft—and the winner has sometimes surprised me!

eBook vs Print Cover Requirements

There are **standard guidelines**, but not a single universal size that works for both eBook and print. Let me break it down:

Feature	eBook Cover	Print Cover
What it includes	Front cover only	Front cover + spine + back cover
Aspect ratio	1.6:1 (taller than wide)	Depends on trim size (e.g., 5×8, 6×9)
Size (Amazon KDP recommended)	2,560 × 1,600 pixels	Varies: based on trim size *and* page count (spine width)
File type	JPEG or TIFF	PDF (print-ready, high resolution, fonts embedded)
Focus	Looks good as a thumbnail on screens	Fits physical dimensions, spine text aligned, back cover info
Tools	Canva, Kindle Previewer, BookBrush	KDP or IngramSpark templates, Canva (print layouts), Atticus, Vellum

Tip for beginners: **Start with your** eBook cover first **(front only). Once you know your trim size and final page count, expand it into a full print cover using the free KDP template.**

How to Use Amazon's Free Cover Template

Amazon makes it easier to design a print cover by giving you a downloadable template. Here's how to use it:

1. **Finish your manuscript first.**
   The page count determines your spine width, so don't design a print cover until editing and formatting are complete.
2. **Go to the KDP Cover Template page.**
   You'll find it on Amazon KDP's help site under "Cover Calculator and Template Generator."
3. **Enter your book details.**
   - Trim size (e.g., 5"×8", 6"×9").
   - Page count (choose the paper type you'll use: white or cream, standard or premium).
   - Binding type (usually paperback).
4. **Download your template.**
   Amazon gives you a ZIP file with both PDF and PNG versions.
5. **Open the template in your design tool.**
   - Canva, Photoshop, GIMP, or BookBrush all work.
   - Place your cover art and text *on top of* the template as a guide.
   - Make sure everything fits within the safe zones (marked areas).
6. **Check the spine.**
   - Keep spine text centred.
   - Don't let images or text bleed into the wrong zones.
   - If your book is under ~100 pages, the spine may be too narrow for text.
7. **Add the back cover details.**
   - Book blurb or tagline.
   - Author bio and photo (optional).
   - ISBN barcode area (leave this blank—Amazon places it for you if you use their free ISBN).
8. **Export as a PDF.**
   Save your file as a high-resolution PDF with embedded fonts, then upload it to KDP.
9. **Preview carefully.**
   Use KDP's print preview tool to check alignment, margins, and how the cover looks as a wraparound. Adjust if needed.

10. **Order a proof copy.**
    Always get a physical proof before approving for sale. It's the best way to catch little details you might miss on screen.

Personal aside: The first time I used Amazon's template, I thought it looked complicated. But once I dropped it into Canva and started layering my design over it, it all made sense—and I actually enjoyed the process!

DIY Options vs Hiring a Designer

When it comes to covers, you've got two main choices: roll up your sleeves and design it yourself, or hire a professional designer. Both options have their place, and the right choice depends on your budget, your goals, and how much you enjoy getting creative.

DIY Options

If you're working on a shoestring budget, the good news is you *can* absolutely design a decent cover yourself. Many successful indie authors do. Here's how:

- **Canva (Free & Paid):** User-friendly, with thousands of templates. Great for beginners. Simply choose a book cover layout, swap fonts and colours, and upload your own images if you want to.
    - *Nonfiction:* Clean, bold templates work best. Think strong titles, uncluttered images.
    - *Fiction:* Canva has genre-specific designs—romance, fantasy, thrillers—that you can tweak.
- **BookBrush (Paid, some free features):** Created specifically for authors. Offers cover templates plus marketing graphics for social media.
- **GIMP (Free):** A free, open-source alternative to Photoshop. Powerful, but with a steeper learning curve.
- **AI Image Tools (Free & Paid):** Can spark ideas or create custom illustrations (great for fantasy maps, symbolic images, or abstract backgrounds).

Budget hack: Start with Canva to create mock-ups. Even if you later hire a designer, these rough drafts will help you communicate your vision.

Hiring a Designer

If you have some budget and prefer to focus on writing, a professional designer can be worth their weight in gold. They'll know what works in your genre, understand visual trends, and create a cover that looks professional even at tiny thumbnail size.

- **Where to find designers:** Fiverr, Upwork, Reedsy, or Facebook author groups.
- **Cost range:** From $50 (basic template-based design) to $500+ for custom artwork.
- **When to consider it:**
    - If your book relies heavily on visuals (e.g., children's books, cookbooks).
    - If design isn't your thing and you'd rather not wrestle with software.
    - If you want a cover that truly stands out in a crowded genre.

A Balanced Approach

You don't have to choose just one path. Many authors start by designing their own covers to save money, then switch to professionals once they can reinvest earnings. Some even blend both—DIYing a simple eBook cover but paying for a polished print cover.

Personal aside: I've found DIY covers not only budget-friendly but enjoyable. It feels like part of the creative journey. That said, I've also seen the value of professional designers when a project needed extra polish. The key is knowing where *you* want to spend your time and money.

Tips for Eye-Catching Covers

A good cover doesn't just "look nice"—it's one of the hardest-working parts of your book. Long before a reader dives into your carefully written chapters, the cover has to do the heavy lifting of grabbing their attention, sparking curiosity, and convincing them that *this* is the book they've been searching for.

Think of it like a shop window display. If it's cluttered, confusing, or poorly put together, people will walk past without a second glance. But if it's inviting, clear, and visually appealing, they'll stop, take notice, and step inside.

Covers also act as a silent promise. They set the tone, signal the genre, and tell readers what kind of experience they can expect—whether that's a spine-tingling thriller, a cosy romance, or a clear and practical how-to guide. A professional-looking cover reassures readers that the inside will be worth their time.

And here's the best part: creating a strong, eye-catching cover doesn't require a huge budget. With today's DIY tools and creative options, even first-time authors can produce designs that stand shoulder-to-shoulder with traditionally published books.

1. Think Small (Thumbnails Matter)

Most readers will first see your book as a thumbnail on Amazon—not full-screen. If the title is hard to read or the image is too busy, your cover won't grab attention.

- **Tip:** Zoom out on your design until it's the size of a postage stamp. Can you still read the title? Does it still stand out?

2. Match Genre Expectations

Every genre has a "look." Readers expect certain colours, fonts, and imagery. Meeting those expectations makes it easier for them to instantly recognise what kind of book yours is.

- **Fiction:**
  - *Romance* → soft colours, elegant fonts, often couples or symbolic objects (like rings or flowers).
  - *Thriller* → dark tones, bold block fonts, moody images like alleyways, shadows, or cityscapes.
  - *Fantasy* → dramatic imagery, ornate fonts, magical symbols, or illustrated worlds.
- **Nonfiction:**
  - *Self-help* → clean, bold fonts, minimal imagery, often bright or calming colours.
  - *Business* → simple, professional covers with strong contrasts and straightforward titles.
  - *Cookbooks/Guides* → large, clear photos and bold, easy-to-read fonts.

3. Prioritise Readability

The title should be the hero of your cover. Subtitles (especially for nonfiction) should also be easy to read. Don't bury them in fancy scripts or overcrowded images.

4. Use Colour Wisely

Colour creates mood.

- Warm colours (reds, oranges) → excitement, urgency.
- Cool colours (blues, greens) → calm, trust, professionalism.
- Contrasts (light on dark, dark on light) → make text pop.

5. Keep It Simple

Resist the urge to cram everything onto the cover. One strong image and clear text is far more powerful than three photos, a swirl of patterns, and six fonts.

Cover Design Checklist

⚠ A Quick Caution:
It's tempting to design a cover that *you* personally love, but remember—the cover isn't for you, it's for your readers. The best covers signal the right genre and appeal directly to the people you want to attract. Always check: *Does this design make sense for my audience?*

Before you finalise your cover, ask yourself:

☑ Can I read the title and subtitle at thumbnail size?
☑ Does the cover instantly signal the genre?
☑ Is the font clean and consistent?
☑ Are the colours balanced and purposeful?
☑ Is the design simple, not cluttered?
☑ Does it look professional compared to bestselling books in my category?

Personal aside: I often create 3–4 different cover drafts and then ask my social media friends which one they prefer. It's fun, it engages your audience, and you might be surprised at which design resonates most!

With your cover complete, you now have the two essentials every book needs: polished words inside and a professional "shop window" outside. Together, they create the package that readers will pick up, click on, or scroll past.

But here's the next big question: *where* will readers actually find your book? A stunning cover and well-formatted interior won't help much if your book isn't available in the right places.

That's where publishing platforms come in. Amazon is the obvious giant in the room, but it's not the only option—and deciding whether to go "Amazon-only" or distribute widely can shape your publishing journey. In the next chapter, we'll explore Kindle Direct Publishing, other retailers like Apple Books and Kobo, and the aggregators that make wide distribution easier. By the end, you'll know exactly which route works best for your goals and budget.

Chapter 7 - Publishing Platforms

You've written, edited, formatted, and designed your book. Now comes the exciting moment when you make it available to the world. But before you hit "publish," you need to decide *where* your book will live.

Self-publishing today offers more choice than ever. The main player, of course, is Amazon, which dominates the eBook market through Kindle Direct Publishing (KDP). Publishing on Amazon is straightforward, free, and gives you access to millions of readers worldwide. For many first-time authors, it's the natural starting point.

But Amazon isn't the only option. Other major retailers, such as Apple Books, Kobo, Barnes & Noble, and Google Play, also have their own readers, often in markets where Amazon is less dominant. And then there are **aggregators** like Draft2Digital and Smashwords, which act as middlemen, distributing your book to multiple platforms simultaneously.

Each option comes with pros and cons. Amazon offers reach and simplicity, but exclusivity rules (like Kindle Unlimited) can limit your flexibility. Going "wide" (publishing on multiple platforms) can increase your audience, but it takes a little more effort to manage.

Personal aside: When I first started, I published on Amazon only—it was the simplest route, and I wanted to learn the ropes. Later, I experimented with wide distribution, which opened my eyes to different reader communities (especially in countries where Kindle isn't the default). Both approaches have their benefits, and the best choice depends on your goals.

In this chapter, we'll explore:

- How Amazon KDP works and what makes it so popular.
- The other major retailers you can publish with.
- Aggregators that simplify wide distribution.
- The pros and cons of exclusivity vs wide publishing.

By the end, you'll know exactly which path suits your book and your budget.

Amazon Kindle Direct Publishing (KDP)

When people talk about self-publishing, they usually mean Amazon. Kindle Direct Publishing (KDP) is the biggest player in the market and the starting point for most indie authors. It's free to use, relatively easy to navigate, and gives your book instant access to millions of readers worldwide.

How KDP Works (Step by Step)

1. **Create an account.** You can log in with your regular Amazon account or set up a separate one for publishing.
2. **Enter your book details.** Title, subtitle, author name, description, categories, and keywords (the metadata we covered earlier).
3. **Upload your manuscript.** For eBooks, you can upload a Word document, EPUB, or Kindle Create file. For print, you'll need a PDF.
4. **Upload your cover.** Either your DIY design or one made by a professional. KDP also has a Cover Creator tool, but it's limited.
5. **Preview your book.** Use the online previewer to check formatting across devices (Kindle Paperwhite, Fire tablet, phone app).
6. **Set pricing and royalty options.** You choose your price, then decide between 35% or 70% royalty (more on this in Chapter 8).
7. **Publish.** Once you hit submit, Amazon usually reviews and approves your book within 72 hours.

Pros of KDP

- **Free to use.** No upfront cost for publishing.
- **Huge audience.** Amazon dominates the eBook market (especially in the US and UK).

- **Print-on-demand included.** You can publish both eBook and paperback through the same platform.
- **Simple interface.** The step-by-step upload process is beginner-friendly.
- **Global reach.** Your book can be sold in multiple Amazon marketplaces worldwide.

Cons of KDP

- **Competition is fierce.** Millions of books are already on Amazon—you'll need good keywords and marketing to stand out.
- **File quirks.** Sometimes formatting looks fine on your computer but odd on Kindle. Always preview carefully.
- **Royalties vary.** The 70% royalty rate has restrictions (e.g., pricing within $2.99–$9.99 USD). Outside that range, you earn only 35%.
- **Exclusivity with Kindle Unlimited.** If you enrol in KDP Select (Amazon's exclusive programme), you can't distribute your eBook elsewhere. This can boost visibility but limits your flexibility.

Personal aside: When I started, I went straight to Amazon KDP. It was free, straightforward, and gave me the thrill of seeing my book live within days. Later, I explored other platforms, but KDP was the best training ground—it taught me the nuts and bolts of publishing without spending a cent.

Other Retailers

While Amazon dominates the eBook market, it isn't the only place readers buy books. Millions of readers around the world use other platforms—some because Amazon isn't as dominant in their country, others because they prefer different devices. Publishing "wide" means making your book available across these outlets, giving you more reach and more potential sales.

Here are the main players:

Apple Books

- **About:** Apple's eBook store, built into every iPhone, iPad, and Mac. Huge potential audience, especially in countries where Apple devices are common.
- **Pros:** Large, loyal customer base; great for nonfiction and lifestyle books; strong global presence.
- **Cons:** Uploading directly requires a Mac (though you can use an aggregator if you're on PC).
- **Best for:** Authors writing nonfiction, business, or lifestyle titles; also works well for fiction in popular genres.

Kobo

- **About:** Big in Canada, Europe, and parts of Asia. Kobo eReaders are sold in many bookstores.
- **Pros:** Strong partnerships with physical bookstores; Kobo Plus (their subscription service) is growing.
- **Cons:** Not as widely used in the US or UK compared to Amazon.
- **Best for:** Authors wanting international reach beyond Amazon; romance and mystery do especially well.

Barnes & Noble Press

- **About:** The online publishing arm of Barnes & Noble, the US bookstore chain. Offers eBooks and print-on-demand.
- **Pros:** Direct access to B&N's online store; potential for in-store placement if your book does well.
- **Cons:** Mainly US-focused; smaller audience compared to Amazon.
- **Best for:** US authors who want their books available in a trusted, recognisable bookstore brand.

Google Play Books

- **About:** Google's digital bookstore, built into Android devices and accessible via web browsers.

- **Pros:** Huge global reach; great discoverability thanks to Google's search power.
- **Cons:** Their pricing system can be quirky (they apply discounts automatically, which affects royalty calculations).
- **Best for:** Authors targeting international or Android-heavy markets; works for both fiction and nonfiction.

IngramSpark

- **About:** A major print-on-demand and eBook distributor used by both indie and traditional publishers. Known for a wide reach into bookstores and libraries.
- **Pros:** Professional credibility—bookshops and libraries prefer ordering through IngramSpark. Wide distribution options for both print and eBooks. Often seen as the industry standard for non-Amazon publishing.
- **Cons:** Charges setup fees (usually around $49 per title, though they run promotions), and the platform has a steeper learning curve than Amazon KDP.
- **Best for:** Authors who want their books available in bookstores, libraries, or internationally in markets where Amazon is weaker. Especially strong for nonfiction and academic books.

Personal aside: When I first explored IngramSpark, it felt more complex than Amazon KDP, but I quickly realised its value—especially for reaching libraries and international readers who prefer buying through traditional channels.

Publishing to each retailer individually can take time, especially if you're juggling different file formats and dashboards. That's where **aggregators** come in—they act as a middleman, distributing your book to multiple stores at once. In the next section, we'll explore the most popular aggregators and when they make sense.

Aggregators

Publishing directly to each retailer is possible, but it can be time-consuming. You'd need to manage multiple accounts, upload files separately, and keep track of different royalty statements. That's where **aggregators** come in.

An aggregator is a company that acts as a middleman. You upload your book once, and they distribute it to multiple retailers for you. In return, they either take a small cut of your royalties or charge a one-time fee. For many indie authors, especially when starting out, this saves time and headaches.

Personal aside: I have only recently started to use an aggregator. So far, I am very impressed.

Here are the most popular options:

Draft2Digital

- **About:** One of the most popular and user-friendly aggregators. Recently merged with Smashwords.
- **Pros:**
    - Free to upload (they only take ~10% of royalties).
    - Wide distribution: Apple Books, Kobo, Barnes & Noble, library services, and more.
    - Offers free formatting tools that produce clean eBook files.
    - Monthly payments, even if you earn small amounts.
- **Cons:**
    - No distribution to Amazon (you'll need to upload to KDP separately).
- **Best for:** Authors who want simplicity and broad reach without upfront costs.

Smashwords

- **About:** One of the oldest aggregators, now part of Draft2Digital. Still has its own store and unique reach.
- **Pros:**
    - Direct access to the Smashwords store, which has a loyal reader base.
    - Strong in library and academic markets.
- **Cons:**
    - The interface is clunkier compared to Draft2Digital.

- **Best for:** Authors who want every possible outlet covered and don't mind extra admin.

IngramSpark

- **About:** Industry giant for print-on-demand distribution. Used by traditional publishers as well as indies.
- **Pros:**
    - Huge reach: bookstores, libraries, and international markets.
    - Print distribution beyond Amazon (bookshops prefer IngramSpark over KDP).
    - Professional credibility—listing with Ingram looks more "traditional."
- **Cons:**
    - Upload fees (around $49 per title, though they often run promotions).
    - Steeper learning curve for setup.
- **Best for:** Authors serious about wide print distribution, especially nonfiction or books targeting libraries/bookstores.

PublishDrive

- **About:** A newer aggregator with a subscription model instead of royalty share.
- **Pros:**
    - Keeps 100% of royalties (after retailer cuts).
    - Wide distribution, including to niche platforms and international stores.
- **Cons:**
    - Monthly fee ($20+), which can eat into profits for new authors.
- **Best for:** Authors with multiple books already selling consistently, who want to maximise royalties.

Budget tip: For most beginners, **Draft2Digital** is the easiest and most affordable option. Pair it with Amazon KDP for maximum reach with minimum cost.

Publishing to each retailer individually can be rewarding, but it also means creating separate accounts, learning different upload systems, and tracking multiple dashboards for sales and payments. For some authors—especially those just starting out—that's a lot to juggle. The good news is you don't have to. This is where **aggregators** come in. They act as a central hub: you upload your book once, and they distribute it to many retailers on your behalf. It's a time-saver, and for many DIY authors, it makes wide publishing feel much more manageable.

Exclusivity vs Wide Distribution

One of the biggest decisions you'll make as a self-published author is whether to publish **exclusively with Amazon** or go **wide** and distribute your book across multiple retailers. There's no one "right" answer—it depends on your goals, budget, and how much effort you want to put into marketing.

Here's how the two approaches compare:

Exclusive with Amazon (KDP Select / Kindle Unlimited)

- **How it works:**
  Enrol your eBook in KDP Select, which means Amazon is the only place it's available digitally. In return, your book can be included in Kindle Unlimited (KU), Amazon's subscription reading service.
- **Pros:**
    - Access to Kindle Unlimited, which has millions of subscribers.
    - Higher visibility through Amazon promotions (Countdown Deals, Free Book Promotions).
    - Simpler: one platform, one dashboard, one set of royalties.
- **Cons:**
    - You can't sell your eBook on Apple, Kobo, Google Play, or anywhere else.

- All your eggs are in Amazon's basket—if their algorithms change, your visibility can drop overnight.
- Print books are not exclusive—you can still distribute those elsewhere.
- **Best for:**
New authors wanting simplicity, those writing in genres that perform well in KU (romance, fantasy, mystery), or anyone testing the waters without juggling multiple platforms.

Wide Distribution (Multiple Platforms)

- **How it works:**
Publish your book across many retailers—either directly or through an aggregator like Draft2Digital or IngramSpark.
- **Pros:**
    - Broader reach: your book is available worldwide, across multiple storefronts and devices.
    - Less dependence on Amazon's algorithms.
    - Builds long-term visibility in different markets (Apple, Kobo, Google Play, libraries).
- **Cons:**
    - More complex to manage (multiple dashboards unless using an aggregator).
    - Slower growth—Amazon readers tend to buy more books, so wide sales may take longer to build.
    - You miss out on Kindle Unlimited readers.
- **Best for:**
Authors looking to build a long-term career, those writing nonfiction (where readers shop beyond Amazon), and anyone who wants true independence from a single retailer.

Which Should You Choose?

- If you want **simplicity, speed, and access to Kindle Unlimited**, go exclusive with Amazon (at least for your first 90 days—you can opt out later).
- If you want **long-term growth, international reach, and more control**, go wide.

Personal aside: I began exclusively with Amazon—it was simple, and KU gave me my first real readers. Later, I shifted to wide distribution for some books, and while growth was slower, it felt good knowing my books were reaching readers beyond Amazon's walls.

With publishing platforms covered, you're now ready to tackle another key part of the process: **Pricing and Royalties**. In the next chapter, we'll explore how to set the right price for your book, how royalties actually work, and how to use promotions to your advantage.

Chapter 8 - Pricing and Royalties

You've written, polished, and packaged your book. It's almost ready to go out into the world—but before you hit "publish," there's another important decision to make: *how much should you charge for it?*

Pricing can feel tricky for new authors. Too high, and readers may hesitate to take a chance on you. Too low, and you risk undervaluing your work—or worse, leaving money on the table. The good news is there are tried-and-tested strategies for setting a price that works for both you and your readers.

At the same time, it's essential to understand **royalties**—how much you'll actually earn from each sale. Different platforms (Amazon, Apple, Kobo, IngramSpark) take different percentages, and the rates can change depending on your pricing choices. Knowing these details upfront helps you make smart decisions that maximise both reach and income.

Personal aside: I remember feeling nervous the first time I had to set a price. I didn't want to scare readers away, but I also wanted to honour the effort I'd put in. Over time, I learned that pricing isn't about guessing—it's about strategy.

In this chapter, we'll explore:

- How royalties work on Amazon KDP and other platforms.
- Strategies for setting the right price for eBooks and paperbacks.
- Free promotions and Kindle Unlimited royalties.
- Why experimenting with pricing can be part of your long-term success.

By the end, you'll feel confident not only about what to charge but also about how to make your pricing work for your publishing goals.

How Royalties Work on KDP

Amazon KDP offers two royalty options for eBooks: **35%** and **70%**. The one you get depends mainly on your book's price and the territories you sell in. It sounds confusing at first, but once you see the numbers, it's straightforward.

The 70% Royalty Option

- Available if your book is priced between **$2.99 and $9.99 USD** (or equivalent in other currencies).
- You earn 70% of the list price **minus a small delivery fee** (based on file size).
- Example:
    - Price: $4.99
    - Royalty: $4.99 × 70% = $3.49
    - Delivery fee: $0.05 (for a text-only file, around 1MB)
    - **Your earnings: $3.44 per sale**

Tip: Text-only books (like most novels and guides) have tiny delivery fees. Image-heavy books (cookbooks, children's books) can lose more to delivery costs, so keep images optimised.

The 35% Royalty Option

- Applies if your book is priced below $2.99 or above $9.99.
- You also get 35% if you sell in countries not covered by the 70% option.
- Example:
    - Price: $1.99
    - Royalty: $1.99 × 35% = **$0.70 per sale**

Tip: If you want to run low-price promotions (like $0.99), expect lower royalties during that time. That said, cheap promotions can boost visibility and reviews, which may pay off later.

Paperbacks on KDP

For print books, the calculation is a little different:

- Royalty is **60% of the list price** (for sales on Amazon).
- Printing cost is subtracted before you're paid.
- Example:
    - Price: $12.99
    - Royalty: $12.99 × 60% = $7.79
    - Printing cost (say $4.50 for a 200-page black-and-white paperback)
    - **Your earnings: $3.29 per sale**

Why This Matters

Understanding royalties isn't just about knowing what you'll earn—it also helps you set smart prices. Many new authors think lower prices automatically mean more sales, but if you price below $2.99, you cut your earnings by half (from 70% to 35%). Sometimes pricing slightly higher not only increases your royalty per sale but also signals more value to readers.

Personal aside: I remember pricing my first eBook at $1.99, thinking it would be more appealing. What I didn't realise was that I was earning less than half of what I could have. When I raised the price to $3.99, I not only earned more but actually sold better—readers often assume higher prices mean higher quality.

Now that you know how royalties work, the next step is setting your **pricing strategy**—finding that sweet spot between attracting readers and making a fair return on your work.

Pricing Strategies

Pricing your book isn't just about covering costs—it's about positioning. The number you choose tells readers how to perceive your work. Too low, and you risk suggesting it isn't worth much; too high, and you might price yourself out of impulse buys. The right strategy depends on your genre, your goals, and where you are in your publishing journey.

1. Pricing eBooks

Most indie authors find success pricing between **$2.99 and $5.99**—low enough to attract new readers but high enough to signal quality and maximise Amazon's 70% royalty.

Typical ranges by genre:

- **Romance & Mystery/Thrillers:** $2.99–$4.99
    - Fast-moving genres where readers often binge series. Lower prices encourage volume sales.
- **Fantasy & Sci-Fi:** $3.99–$5.99
    - Readers expect more world-building and longer books, so they accept slightly higher prices.
- **Nonfiction (self-help, how-to, business):** $4.99–$9.99
    - Practical books are often seen as "investments." Readers will pay more if the book promises real value.

Examples:

- A cosy mystery author might launch Book 1 at $2.99 to attract new readers, then price later books in the series at $3.99–$4.99.
- A nonfiction parenting guide might comfortably launch at $6.99, since the audience is willing to pay for trusted advice.

DIY Tip: Check the top 20 books in your Amazon category. See what's selling and position yourself within that range.

2. Pricing Paperbacks

Paperbacks are naturally more expensive due to printing costs. Readers know this and are willing to pay more than for an eBook.

Typical ranges by genre:

- **Fiction paperbacks:** $9.99–$14.99
- **Nonfiction guides/manuals:** $12.99–$19.99
- **Workbooks, cookbooks, or illustrated books:** $14.99–$29.99 (printing costs are higher for colour and images)

Examples:

- A 250-page romance novel might sell at **$12.99**.
- A 180-page self-publishing guide could be priced at **$14.99**.
- A colour photography book might need to be **$24.99** to cover costs.

Budget note: Always run your price through the KDP royalty calculator before finalising. You don't want to set a price that leaves you with pennies after printing costs.

3. Launch Strategies

Your first price doesn't have to be your forever price. Many indie authors use launch strategies to build momentum:

- **Low Launch Price:** Start at $0.99–$2.99 for the first week or month to attract early readers and reviews. Then raise to your "real" price once sales pick up.
- **Permafree First in Series:** If you're writing fiction series, making Book 1 permanently free can hook readers and drive sales of later books.
- **Introductory Discount:** For nonfiction, launch at a lower price (say, $2.99–$3.99) to encourage reviews, then raise to $6.99+ once credibility builds.

4. Experimenting with Price

The beauty of self-publishing is flexibility. You can change your price at any time to test what works.

- Drop your price temporarily to boost downloads.
- Raise it if you feel you're undervaluing your work.
- Track results (sales, reviews, rankings) to see how readers respond.

Real-world example:

- An author priced her eBook at $1.99 for six months with steady but modest sales. When she raised it to $4.99, she sold slightly fewer copies—but her income doubled because of the higher royalty rate.

5. Perception of Value

Readers associate price with quality. A $0.99 eBook might look like a bargain, but it can also look like "cheap and cheerful." A $4.99 price suggests the book has real substance. For nonfiction in particular, higher prices often build trust.

Personal aside: I've learned not to be afraid of pricing slightly higher. Readers are often willing to pay more than you expect, especially if the cover, blurb, and reviews all promise quality. Undervaluing your work can hurt more than help.

Promotions and Kindle Unlimited

Pricing sets the stage, but promotions give your book momentum. They help you get noticed in a crowded marketplace, attract reviews, and sometimes trigger Amazon's algorithms to recommend your book to more readers. If you enrol in Amazon's **KDP Select** programme (which requires exclusivity), you unlock two powerful tools: **Free Promotions** and **Kindle Countdown Deals**. Plus, you gain access to **Kindle Unlimited (KU)**, Amazon's subscription reading service.

Free Promotions

- You can set your eBook price to **free** for up to 5 days every 90 days.
- Great for boosting downloads and visibility. A surge of free downloads can help your book climb Amazon charts, which may attract more paid buyers afterward.

Example: A new mystery author makes Book 1 in her series free for three days. Thousands of readers download it, and many go on to buy Book 2 and Book 3 at full price.

Tip: Plan your free days around a marketing push—announce them on social media, newsletters, or free book promotion sites.

Kindle Countdown Deals

- Temporarily discount your book (e.g., $4.99 down to $1.99) for up to 7 days.
- Readers see the original price crossed out, which creates urgency.
- You keep the **70% royalty rate**, even though the price is below $2.99 (a perk only available during Countdown Deals).

Example: A self-help author runs a Kindle Countdown Deal at $1.99, paired with a social media campaign. Sales spike during the week, boosting visibility and reviews.

Kindle Unlimited (KU)

- KU is a subscription service where readers pay monthly to read as many books as they want.
- Instead of earning royalties per sale, you're paid based on **pages read**. The rate changes monthly, but usually hovers around $0.004–$0.005 per page.
- Example: A 300-page novel read cover-to-cover earns about $1.20–$1.50 from KU.

Pros:

- Access to millions of voracious readers (especially romance, fantasy, and mystery fans).
- Page reads can add up quickly, sometimes rivaling or surpassing outright sales.

Cons:

- Exclusivity: while enrolled in KU, your eBook can't be sold on Apple, Kobo, or Google Play.
- Income can fluctuate—some months, KU payouts are lower.

Personal aside: When I first tried Kindle Unlimited, I was surprised by how many readers came through page reads rather than outright sales. For fiction especially, it can be a fantastic way to build a following. But I also like the freedom of wide distribution—so I've experimented with both approaches, depending on the book.

Promotions and KU can give your book a powerful boost, especially in the early days when you're trying to get noticed among millions of other titles. A well-timed free promo can flood your book into readers' hands, a countdown deal can create urgency that drives sales, and Kindle Unlimited can steadily build income through page reads even if your sales are modest. Together, these tools can act like a launchpad—helping your book climb the rankings, gather those all-important first reviews, and gain visibility beyond your immediate circle.

But promotions are just the beginning. Smart publishing means keeping an eye on what's working, adjusting when needed, and being willing to experiment. In the next section, we'll look at how to **track your sales and refine your strategy**, so you can build steady momentum long after launch day.

Tracking and Adjusting

Publishing your book is just the beginning. Once it's live, the real work is watching how it performs and making small tweaks to keep sales moving. Luckily, you don't need complicated spreadsheets or expensive software to track progress—most of what you need is built right into the platforms you're publishing on.

Amazon KDP Reports

Amazon gives you a sales dashboard where you can see:

- **Units sold** (by day, week, or month).
- **Royalties earned** (broken down by marketplace, e.g., US, UK, Canada).
- **Kindle Unlimited page reads.**
- **Print sales** (paperbacks or hardcovers).

Tip: Don't obsess over daily sales. Look at weekly or monthly trends—it gives a clearer picture.

Other Platforms

Apple Books, Kobo, and Google Play all provide similar dashboards with sales and royalty reports. If you use an aggregator like Draft2Digital, you'll see all your data in one place.

What to Track

- **Sales spikes:** Did you sell more after a promotion or social media post?
- **Price changes:** Did lowering or raising your price affect downloads?
- **Keywords & categories:** If you adjust metadata, do you appear in new charts or rankings?
- **Formats:** Do readers prefer your eBook or paperback?

Making Adjustments

Once you see how your book performs, you can experiment with small changes:

- **Price tweaks:** Try raising or lowering your eBook by $1 to see if it changes sales.
- **Blurb refresh:** Update your description to make it punchier.
- **Cover updates:** If sales are slow, test a new design—sometimes a fresh cover can transform a book's performance.
- **Promotions:** Schedule regular free days or countdown deals to keep momentum alive.

Think Long-Term

Don't panic if your book isn't an overnight bestseller. Most indie authors see sales grow slowly as they release more titles, build an audience, and refine their strategies. Your first book is often your testing ground.

Personal aside: I used to refresh my dashboard constantly, hoping for instant results. Eventually, I learned to step back, look at monthly patterns, and see every book as part of a bigger picture. The tweaks I made along the way—like adjusting prices or running timed promos—taught me more than any "how-to" article.

With pricing, royalties, and promotions in your toolkit, you've now got a solid understanding of how the financial side of self-publishing works. You know what you'll earn per sale, how to position your book's price for your audience, and how to use Amazon's built-in promotions to give your book an early boost. You've also learned that publishing isn't a "set it and forget it" process—it's about tracking results, making adjustments, and treating each change as an experiment that helps you learn what resonates with readers.

But here's the truth: even the best-formatted book with a smart price and polished cover won't sell if nobody knows it exists. That's where marketing comes in. In the next chapter, we'll look at practical, budget-friendly ways to promote your book—without needing a degree in advertising or a huge budget.

Chapter 9 - Marketing Your Book

Writing and publishing your book is a huge achievement—but now comes the part that often feels the most daunting: marketing. Many authors dream that once their book is live on Amazon, readers will magically find it. Sadly, that rarely happens. With millions of titles competing for attention, your book needs a little push to get noticed.

The good news? Marketing doesn't have to mean expensive ad campaigns or complicated strategies. In fact, many of the most effective methods are free or low-cost. At its core, marketing is simply about connecting your book with the readers who are most likely to love it.

Think of it this way: if writing the book was about telling your story, marketing is about inviting people to read it. It's sharing, not shouting. And when you approach it with that mindset, it becomes far less intimidating.

Personal aside: When I first started, the word "marketing" made me nervous. I pictured glossy adverts and pushy sales tactics—not my style at all. But over time, I discovered that simple things, like talking about my book on social media or sharing the writing journey with friends, were forms of marketing too. Once I reframed it as connection, it felt natural—and even fun.

In this chapter, we'll explore:

- The basics of building your author brand.
- How to use social media without it taking over your life.
- Free and low-cost ways to spread the word about your book.
- When (and if) to consider paid advertising.

By the end, you'll have a toolbox of practical strategies to help your book find its readers—without burning out or breaking the bank.

Building Your Author Brand

Before you dive into social media posts or advertising, it's worth stepping back and thinking about your **author brand**. This isn't about creating a fake persona or hiring a marketing team—it's simply about deciding how you want readers to see you.

Your brand is the impression you leave behind. It's built from your covers, your tone of voice, your website or social media presence, and even the way you interact with readers. Done well, it makes you memorable and helps readers trust that your next book will deliver the experience they're looking for.

What Makes Up an Author Brand?

- **Your Name:** Will you publish under your real name, a pen name, or both? (Tip: stick to one name per genre to avoid confusing readers.)
- **Your Covers:** Consistent design elements help readers recognise your books.
- **Your Voice:** The way you speak in blurbs, newsletters, or posts—serious and professional, warm and friendly, or quirky and fun.
- **Your Online Presence:** A simple website, an author page on Amazon, or a Facebook page can all be part of your "shopfront."

Fiction Example

Imagine a cosy mystery writer whose stories are filled with small-town charm, eccentric neighbours, and gentle humour. Their author brand might include:

- **Playful covers** with illustrated cottages, pawprints, or steaming teacups that instantly signal "cosy mystery."
- **A light-hearted author bio** that mentions their love of detective shows, baking scones, or tending to their garden—tying their real life to the tone of their books.
- **Social media posts** featuring snapshots of their writing desk with a cat sprawled across the keyboard, polls like *"Which*

biscuit would my sleuth eat first?", or photos of a picturesque village that inspired a setting.

Everything they share reinforces the same message: these books are warm, fun, and comforting. Readers begin to associate the author with that cosy world and feel like they're part of it, even outside the pages of the novel.

Fantasy Fiction Example

Think of a fantasy author whose novels feature sprawling kingdoms, magical quests, and richly imagined worlds. Their brand might include:

- **Epic, dramatic covers** with sweeping landscapes, glowing swords, or mysterious runes—instantly signalling "fantasy adventure."
- **An author bio** that leans into the genre: perhaps mentioning a lifelong love of Tolkien, Dungeons & Dragons, or wandering castle ruins on holiday.
- **Social media posts** that feed reader imagination:
  - Short world-building snippets (e.g., "Did you know the palace in my book was inspired by a real medieval fortress in France?").
  - Fun "what if" polls like *"If you had to choose, would you carry a sword, staff, or spellbook?"*
  - Behind-the-scenes sketches or AI-generated images of their characters or settings.

All of this reinforces the sense of wonder and immersion readers expect from fantasy—and helps the author attract the exact audience who loves to escape into new worlds.

Nonfiction Example

Now picture a self-help author writing about stress management. Their brand might include:

- **Clean, professional covers** with bold titles and calm colours (like blues and greens) that signal clarity and trust.
- **Encouraging, straightforward language** in their author bio—highlighting experience, passion for helping others, and a tone of reassurance.
- **Social media posts** that share practical, bite-sized value:
    - A quick breathing exercise for busy mornings.
    - An inspirational quote with a short reflection.
    - A behind-the-scenes note: *"Here's the journal I kept while testing these strategies."*

This consistency positions the author as approachable, reliable, and supportive—exactly what readers want from a self-help guide. Over time, followers come to see them as a trusted voice in the field.

Takeaway: Whether cosy mystery, self-help, or epic fantasy, the principle is the same: **align your covers, bio, and online presence with the experience your book delivers.** That way, your brand feels authentic and instantly recognisable.

Practical Steps to Start

1. Google yourself (or your pen name). What shows up? That's already part of your brand.
2. Write a short author bio—friendly but professional—that you can use everywhere.
3. Create a simple landing page or use Amazon's free Author Central to manage your profile.
4. Think about 2–3 themes you'd like to be known for (e.g., "cosy, witty mysteries" or "practical, supportive self-help").

Personal aside: I didn't think of myself as having a "brand" at first—it felt too corporate. But once I realised it was simply about consistency (my tone, the way I show up online, and the covers I design), it clicked. Readers appreciate knowing what to expect, and that's really all branding is.

Mini Exercise: Define Your Author Brand

1. **Choose 3 words** that capture the "vibe" of your book.

- For cosy mystery: *playful, charming, light-hearted.*
- For self-help: *calm, supportive, professional.*
- For fantasy: *epic, magical, adventurous.*

2. **Match those words** to elements of your brand:
   - *Covers:* What colours, fonts, or imagery reflect your vibe?
   - *Bio:* How can you phrase your author story to reinforce those qualities?
   - *Social media:* What kind of posts would feel natural with that tone?
3. **Test it out.** Draft a short social post or mock up a cover idea based on your three words. Does it feel consistent with your book?

The goal isn't to force yourself into a box—it's to create a **cohesive impression** so readers instantly understand what your work is about.

Free and Low-Cost Marketing Strategies

Marketing doesn't have to mean spending hundreds of dollars on Facebook ads or hiring a PR team. In fact, some of the most effective strategies for indie authors are either free or cost very little. What matters most isn't the size of your budget, but your willingness to be consistent and a little creative.

Think of marketing as planting seeds. Each post, email, or conversation is a seed that could grow into a new reader, a review, or even a long-term fan. The key is to plant steadily and nurture those connections over time. The results may not be instant, but they build momentum that lasts far beyond launch week.

The best part? These grassroots methods often feel more natural and personal. Instead of shouting "buy my book!" to strangers, you're sharing your work with communities, readers, and networks who genuinely want to hear from you. And that kind of connection is not only effective—it's enjoyable.

1. Use Your Existing Network

- Tell family, friends, and colleagues about your book.
- Share the news on your personal social media accounts.
- Don't be shy—most people are excited to support someone they know.

Tip: Ask them to leave honest reviews on Amazon or Goodreads. Those first reviews are gold.

2. Build an Email List

An email list is one of the most powerful tools an author can have. Even a small list of readers who enjoy your work gives you a direct line to people who are most likely to buy your next book.

- Start with a simple free service like MailerLite or Mailchimp.
- Offer a free short story (fiction) or a useful checklist (nonfiction) as a sign-up incentive.

3. Engage in Reader Communities

- Join Facebook groups or Reddit communities focused on your genre.
- Contribute genuinely to discussions rather than spamming links.
- Share your journey, insights, or recommendations—then mention your book naturally when relevant.

4. Goodreads Presence

Goodreads is where passionate readers hang out.

- Claim your author profile (free).
- List your books and link them to your Amazon page.
- Join groups or run giveaways (budget-friendly promo options).

5. Collaborate with Other Authors

- Do newsletter swaps—recommend each other's books to your readers.
- Run joint promotions (especially if you write in similar genres).
- Share experiences and tips—writing communities thrive on support.

6. Book Promotion Sites (Free & Low-Cost)

- There are websites where you can submit your free or discounted book to get extra visibility. Examples: Freebooksy, Book Cave, Book Rebel.
- Some are free, others charge a small fee ($10–$50).

7. Local Opportunities

- Offer to speak at libraries, book clubs, or community groups.
- Donate a copy of your book to local libraries.
- Approach independent bookstores—some are happy to stock local authors or host signings.

Personal aside: Some of my best feedback has come from local readers who discovered my books in community spaces. Never underestimate the power of word-of-mouth—it's still one of the strongest marketing tools out there.

These grassroots strategies not only save money but also help you build genuine connections with readers. Once you've mastered these, you can consider scaling up with paid ads or more advanced campaigns—but you may be surprised how far free and low-cost methods can take you.

Social Media: Pros and Cons (Free vs Paid Ads)

Social media can be a wonderful tool for authors—but it can also become overwhelming if you don't approach it with clear goals. It's important to know the difference between free, organic use of social platforms and paid advertising, and what each can realistically do for you.

Free / Organic Social Media

This is everything you do without spending money—posting updates, sharing your book cover, joining groups, or chatting with readers.

Pros:

- No cost—just your time.
- Builds genuine connections with readers and other authors.
- Lets you share your writing journey, personality, and interests.
- Great for long-term community building.

Cons:

- Growth can be slow—followers don't appear overnight.
- Algorithms often limit how many people see your posts.
- Requires consistency to be effective (posting 1–3 times a week at least).

Best for: Beginners and authors on a budget who enjoy engaging with readers in a natural, low-pressure way.

Paid Social Media Ads

Platforms like Facebook, Instagram, Amazon, and TikTok allow you to pay for ads that target specific audiences (by age, location, interests, or reading habits).

Pros:

- Can reach thousands of potential readers quickly.
- Lets you target very specific groups (e.g., "women aged 35–55 who read cosy mysteries").

- Scales—if an ad works, you can increase budget for bigger reach.

Cons:

- Costs money (Facebook and Amazon ads can burn through cash if not managed carefully).
- Steep learning curve—you may need to test multiple ads before finding one that converts.
- Results aren't guaranteed—an ad may not sell as many books as you hope.

Best for: Authors who already have a polished product (great cover, strong blurb, good reviews) and some budget to invest.

Finding a Balance

Most indie authors start with free, organic posting to build awareness and community. Once you have your foundation—an audience that responds to your content and a book that's polished and reviewed—you might consider testing small ad campaigns. Even $20–$50 can give you valuable insight into which audiences respond to your book.

Personal aside: I found that free posting kept me grounded and connected, while small paid ads (carefully tested) gave my books an extra push during promotions or launches. The two work best together—not as either/or.

A Simple Marketing Plan

Marketing doesn't have to be overwhelming or complicated. You don't need dozens of tools, a huge budget, or hours each day on social media. What you do need is a simple, repeatable plan that fits into your life and helps readers discover your book. Here's a framework you can adapt:

1. Build Your Foundations

- Set up your **Amazon Author Page** (free).
- Create a simple **website or landing page** where readers can learn more about you.
- Write a short, engaging **author bio** you can use everywhere.

2. Nurture Your Audience

- Pick **one or two social media platforms** that feel natural to you.
- Post 2–3 times per week (snippets, behind-the-scenes, quotes, or tips).
- Engage—reply to comments, ask questions, and treat it like a conversation.

3. Use Free Tools

- Encourage readers to **leave reviews**—they're powerful social proof.
- Join genre-specific **Facebook groups, Goodreads groups, or forums.**
- Swap mentions with fellow authors—recommend each other's books.

4. Plan Simple Promotions

- Schedule **free days** or **countdown deals** on Amazon if you're in KDP Select.
- Submit your book to free or low-cost promo sites (like Freebooksy or Book Cave).
- Share promotions with your email list and social media followers.

5. Experiment with Small Ads (Optional)

- Once your book has a solid cover, blurb, and reviews, test a small ad budget ($20–$50).
- Try one platform (Facebook, Amazon, or BookBub), track results, and only scale if it works.

6. Track and Adjust

- Check your sales dashboard weekly or monthly.
- Note which posts, promos, or price changes led to bumps in sales.
- Do more of what works, and drop what doesn't—don't waste energy forcing strategies you dislike.

Personal aside: My best results have always come from keeping things simple. When I tried to do "everything," I ended up exhausted. But by focusing on a few steady habits—posting, running occasional promos, and staying connected with readers—I saw far more consistent growth.

With this simple plan, you can market your book without burning out or feeling like you need to master every platform at once. The key is consistency: showing up in small, steady ways that keep your book visible and your readers engaged. Over time, these little efforts stack up—each post, review, or promo adds another brick to the foundation of your author career.

Remember, marketing isn't about shouting the loudest—it's about building trust and connection. Readers who discover you through these grassroots methods are far more likely to stick around for your next book, and the one after that.

In the next chapter, we'll look beyond the launch and talk about **the long game**: how to keep momentum going, how to think about your next project, and how to build a sustainable publishing journey that grows with you.

Chapter 10 - The Long Game: Building a Publishing Career

Publishing your first book is a huge milestone. But here's the secret many new authors don't realise: one book is just the beginning. The real magic happens when you start to think about the *long game*.

The truth is, very few authors make a career from a single title. Success usually comes from building a catalogue of books, each one reinforcing the others and helping new readers discover you. It's about momentum—every book you publish adds to your visibility, credibility, and income.

The long game also means treating your writing life as a journey rather than a one-off project. Instead of obsessing over overnight success, focus on steady growth: learning new skills, experimenting with different strategies, and building a loyal readership who come back for more.

Personal aside: When I published my first book, I thought the hard work was over. In reality, it was the first step. Over time, I discovered that writing consistently—not perfectly, but consistently—was what built my confidence, my brand, and eventually my audience.

In this chapter, we'll explore:

- Why publishing more than one book is the best marketing strategy you'll ever have.
- How to plan your next project without burning out.
- Building systems and habits for a sustainable writing life.
- Balancing creativity with the business side of being an author.

By the end, you'll see how self-publishing isn't just about getting *a* book out into the world—it's about building a career, if that's the path you choose.

Why More Than One Book Matters

If publishing your first book feels like climbing a mountain, publishing your second might feel like climbing a whole new one. But here's the truth: the second (and third, and fourth) book is where your author career really begins to take shape.

One book is a milestone. Two books start a catalogue. Three or more give readers a reason to stick around. Each new release not only has the potential to attract fresh readers, but also breathes new life into your earlier titles.

For Fiction Authors

Readers love series. If someone enjoys Book 1, they're far more likely to buy Book 2 and Book 3 than to take a gamble on a brand-new author they've never heard of. The more books you have available, the easier it becomes to keep readers within your "world."

- **Example:** A cosy mystery author launches with one book and sees modest sales. But when Book 2 comes out, readers who enjoyed the first story eagerly buy the second. By Book 3, new readers who discover the series binge-read the entire set, multiplying sales of earlier titles.

Tip: Even if you write standalones, try to keep them within a consistent genre. That way, readers who liked one will trust that the next will deliver a similar experience.

For Nonfiction Authors

A single nonfiction book can position you as knowledgeable, but multiple books establish you as an authority. Each book can tackle a different angle of your subject, or branch into related topics.

- **Example:** A wellness coach starts with a book on stress management. Later, they publish a companion journal, followed by a book on building resilience. Together, the three books create a "mini-library" that appeals to the same audience—and gives readers more reasons to buy again.

⬦ *Tip:* Think about your book not just as a single product but as the first piece of a larger body of work. Over time, your books can cross-promote one another, multiplying your reach.

The Compounding Effect

Every new book you publish is like another hook in the water. Some readers will find you through your latest release, others through your first, but once they've enjoyed one, they often move on to the rest. That's why seasoned indie authors often say, *"The best marketing for your first book is your second book."*

Planning Your Next Project

After the thrill (and exhaustion) of publishing your first book, it can feel daunting to think about the next one. But planning your next project doesn't have to mean diving straight into another marathon. The key is balance: keeping momentum without burning yourself out.

1. Take Stock First

- Celebrate your achievement—finishing and publishing a book is no small thing!
- Reflect on what worked in your process and what didn't. Did you enjoy writing daily, or were weekly sessions more realistic? Did editing drag on too long? Use those lessons to shape your next approach.

2. Stay in Your Lane (for Now)

- **Fiction:** If your first book was part of a series, your next project almost writes itself—carry on with Book 2. If it was a standalone, consider another story in the same genre so readers know what to expect.
- **Nonfiction:** Think about follow-ups that deepen or expand on your first book. A companion journal, a workbook, or a

second title tackling a related topic can help you build authority.

Tip: Consistency builds trust. Once you've got several books under your belt, you can experiment with new genres or niches.

3. Outline Early

Don't wait until you're knee-deep in writing to decide where the book is going. Spend time upfront creating a roadmap.

- *Fiction:* Sketch your characters, plot arcs, and key turning points.
- *Nonfiction:* Draft a table of contents and bullet-point the main takeaways for each chapter.

Even a loose plan saves a lot of stress later.

4. Pace Yourself

It's tempting to dive straight back in, but burnout is real. Give yourself breathing space.

- Set manageable goals (e.g., 500 words per day or one chapter per week).
- Build writing time into your life instead of forcing your life around writing.

5. Think Long-Term

Consider how your next project fits into the bigger picture of your author career.

- Does it build a series?
- Does it reinforce your expertise?
- Does it appeal to the same audience you're already building?

Personal aside: After publishing my first book, I thought I had to rush into the next one. In reality, slowing down to reflect helped me plan smarter. That balance meant the next project wasn't just another book—it was a step forward in my bigger journey as a writer.

Building Sustainable Writing Habits

Publishing a book isn't just about inspiration—it's about consistency. The authors who build lasting careers aren't necessarily the fastest writers or the most talented; they're the ones who find a rhythm that works for them and stick with it over the long term. Sustainable habits protect you from burnout, help you finish projects, and keep the joy in your writing.

1. Know Your Natural Rhythm

Not everyone is a "write every day" author. Some people thrive on daily sessions, while others do better with longer bursts on weekends.

- **Morning writer?** Protect an hour before work.
- **Night owl?** Write after the household quiets down.
- **Busy schedule?** Aim for 2–3 focused sessions per week.

Tip: Consistency matters more than word count. Even 500 words a day adds up to 182,500 words a year—enough for multiple books.

2. Set Manageable Goals

- Break your project into milestones: outline, first draft, self-edit, etc.
- Use word count or time goals that feel achievable.
- Celebrate small wins—finishing a chapter is progress worth noting!

3. Create a Writing Environment

Make it easy to slip into "writing mode."

- Find a dedicated space (a desk, a corner, even a favourite chair).
- Use rituals—like tea, music, or a particular notebook—to signal it's time to write.
- Eliminate distractions (turn off notifications, use a timer).

4. Balance Writing and Marketing

Marketing is important, but don't let it eat all your creative time. Schedule blocks for writing first, then fit marketing tasks around it. Remember: your next book is the best marketing tool you'll ever have.

5. Protect Your Energy

- Take breaks between projects to recharge.
- Read widely—it fuels creativity.
- Don't compare your pace to others; every writer has their own speed.

6. Build Accountability

- Join a writing group, in person or online.
- Share your goals with a friend or fellow writer.
- Use writing sprints or challenges (like NaNoWriMo) for motivation.

Personal aside: I used to push myself too hard, thinking I had to churn out words daily. Over time, I learned that gentle consistency suited me better. Writing became less of a grind and more of a rhythm I could sustain—and that made all the difference.

Balancing Creativity and Business

For many indie authors, the creative side of writing feels natural—dreaming up stories, shaping characters, or sharing knowledge and experience. The business side, on the other hand—tracking royalties, managing marketing, and thinking about profit—can feel intimidating or even unappealing. But if you want to build a sustainable publishing career, you'll need to balance both.

Think of it this way: the creative side produces the product, and the business side makes sure it finds readers and keeps the lights on. One without the other won't get you very far.

1. Protect Your Creative Time

- Writing is your core task—guard it fiercely.
- Block off regular sessions for drafting and editing.
- Remind yourself: marketing works best when there's more than one book to sell.

2. Keep Business Simple

- Track income and expenses in a basic spreadsheet (royalties, ads, software subscriptions, ISBNs).
- Keep receipts—many costs can be tax-deductible.
- Review your sales monthly, not daily. Patterns matter more than spikes.

3. Separate Roles in Your Mind

- **Writer mode:** creative, playful, imaginative.
- **Publisher mode:** analytical, organised, practical.
- Switching hats can reduce stress—you don't have to be both at once.

4. Reinvest in Your Career

- Start small: reinvest part of your royalties into editing, covers, or marketing for your next book.
- Over time, this creates a virtuous cycle—better books, better sales, more resources for future projects.

5. Remember Why You Write

In the whirlwind of publishing—tweaking metadata, checking dashboards, juggling covers, and chasing reviews—it's easy to forget the simplest truth: you started writing because you had something to say, a story to tell, or an idea worth sharing. That spark is the heart of your author journey, and keeping it alive is what makes all the business tasks worthwhile.

When the numbers feel discouraging or the to-do list overwhelming, pause and reconnect with your *why*. Maybe it's the joy of creating worlds out of nothing, the thrill of helping someone solve a problem, or the dream of leaving behind a book your grandchildren can one day hold in their hands.

Writing is more than sales—it's connection. Even if one reader, somewhere, feels seen, comforted, or entertained by your words, that's an impact worth celebrating.

Practical reminder: Keep a small "why I write" note somewhere you can see it—on your desk, in your journal, or even as a screensaver. On tough days, reading it can bring you back to centre.

Personal aside: There have been moments when I've felt lost in the business side—wondering if all the effort was worth it. But each time I received a message from a reader saying my words had touched them, it reminded me: *this is why I write.* The numbers matter, but the connection matters more.

Conclusion - Your Words Matter

By now, you've walked through the entire self-publishing process—from that very first spark of an idea, through drafting, editing, formatting, covers, ISBNs, platforms, pricing, marketing, and beyond. You've seen the tools, the choices, the pros and cons. You know where to save money, where to invest, and how to avoid the common traps that trip up new authors.

But here's the most important takeaway: you don't have to do it all perfectly, and you don't have to do it all at once. Self-publishing is a journey, not a race. Every book teaches you something new, every promotion gives you fresh insights, and every reader you reach is proof that your words matter.

The beauty of self-publishing is control—you get to decide your path. Maybe your goal is to publish one book as a passion project. Maybe it's to build a career with a shelf full of titles. Either way, the tools and opportunities are in your hands.

Remember your why. It's easy to get caught up in sales numbers, algorithms, and deadlines. But at the heart of it all, you write because you have something to share—whether that's a thrilling story, a practical solution, or a piece of your own experience. Keep that spark alive, and it will carry you through the ups and downs of the publishing journey.

Personal aside: Looking back, my proudest moments haven't been dashboards or royalty checks—it's been the emails from readers who said my book gave them comfort, laughter, or clarity. That's the kind of success no graph can measure.

So take a deep breath, pat yourself on the back, and remember: you are now a published author. And that's something no one can take away from you.

The next step? Keep writing, keep learning, and keep sharing your words with the world.

Proofreading Mini-Checklist

Before hitting "publish," run through this quick list:

- ☐ Typos and spelling mistakes.

- ☐ Missing or extra punctuation (especially quotation marks).

- ☐ Consistent formatting (fonts, spacing, margins).

- ☐ Chapter headings and numbers match the table of contents.

- ☐ Page breaks are clean at the start of each chapter.

- ☐ Consistent use of italics and bold (e.g., book titles italicised).

- ☐ Check figures, tables, or images are labelled correctly.

- ☐ No "widows" or "orphans" (stray words/lines on a page).

- ☐ Proofread the final pages carefully (typos love hiding there!).

About the Author

Fee O'Shea is a multi-genre author who delights in weaving stories and ideas into books that inspire, entertain, and inform. With a background that spans creative writing, activism, and a lifelong love of learning, Fee has embraced self-publishing as both a craft and a calling.

Over the years, Fee has written across fiction and nonfiction—cosy mysteries, self-help guides, and practical "how-to" books—all with the same goal: to connect with readers in a way that feels honest, helpful, and a little bit fun. A self-confessed book lover from an early age, Fee has always believed that words have the power to change lives, whether through laughter, comfort, or practical wisdom.

When she's not writing, Fee is often found sketching, creating digital art, or working on her other creative projects. She also enjoys travel, improv theatre, and spending time with her growing family.

Fee's self-publishing journey began the same way yours may be starting now—with one idea, a blank page, and a determination to share it with the world. She continues to explore and refine the process, and hopes that by sharing her experience, she can encourage other budding authors to do the same.

Author's note: "Self-publishing has given me freedom—not just to write, but to share my work on my own terms. I hope this book has shown you that you can do it too, without fear, without spending a fortune, and with the confidence that your words matter."

www.ingramcontent.com/pod-product-compliance
Lightning Source LLC
Chambersburg PA
CBHW062040290426
44109CB00026B/2684